T0326538

Value of Failure

Value of Failure

The Spectrum of Challenges for the Economy

Edited by
Joanna Markiewicz and Leszek Gracz

Union Bridge Books

UNION BRIDGE BOOKS

An imprint of Wimbledon Publishing Company Limited (WPC)

First published in the United Kingdom in 2017 by Union Bridge Books

This edition first published in UK and USA 2017
UNION BRIDGE BOOKS
75–76 Blackfriars Road
London SE1 8HA
www.unionbridgebooks.com

British Library Cataloguing-in-Publication Data
A catalogue record for this book is available from the British Library.

ISBN-13: 978-1-78308-733-4 (Hbk)
ISBN-10: 1-78308-733-1 (Hbk)

ISBN-13: 978-1-78308-734-1 (Pbk)
ISBN-10: 1-78308-734-X (Pbk)

This title is also available as an e-book.

This reviewed publication has been funded with support from the European Commission.

The authors are solely responsible for this publication (communication) and neither the
Commission nor National Agency for Erasmus+ programme accept responsibility for any
use that may be made of the information contained therein.

The publication is co-financed by the Ministry of Science and Higher Education, Poland.

The publication is co-financed by Erasmus+ programme.

CONTENTS

ILLUSTRATIONS

Figures

Tables

Charts

PREFACE

Growing levels of education, the increasing availability of capital, the diversification and specialization of economic activities and the numerous soft and hard supports available to start new businesses have led to the creation of more and more micro and small businesses across Europe. But while the process of setting up a business is increasingly straightforward, keeping it going is much tougher. In normal times, business entry and business exit are natural processes, inherent to economic life. In fact, 50 percent of enterprises do not survive the first five years and, of all business closures, bankruptcies account in average for 15 percent (*A Second Chance for Entrepreneurs*, Expert Group Report 2011). Yet, the number of bankruptcies peaked during the recent financial crisis and even before that, the Lisbon Partnership had identified the key role of "overcoming the stigma of business failure" as a strategy for growth and jobs.

There are clear economic and social rationales to promoting a second chance for failed entrepreneurs and deriving positive experience from negative situations. First and foremost, businesses set up by restarters grow faster than first-timers in terms of turnover and jobs created (Stam, Audretsch, Meijaard 2006), and approximately one-fifth of all successful business people failed the first time around. The case studies of Ford, Hershey and Disney are instructive for young entrepreneurs in this matter.

Second, most of the time, business failure is not due to the incompetence of the entrepreneurs but due to external circumstances, such as a slump in demand, a financial crisis or the rise of a new competitor. However, this professional failure is often confused with personal failure, and low self-esteem causes individuals to withdraw and retreat to safer employment options.

Third, it is accepted that a society does not generate innovation and productivity by steadfastly avoiding mistakes but, rather, by learning from them. Yet our culture and incentive system does not reflect this. There is much evidence to show that Europeans as a whole are relatively risk-averse, especially compared to countries such as the United States. In Germany, for example, only 1–2 percent of new companies annually are founded by second-chance entrepreneurs (see KfW-Gründungsmonitor 2013), and the World Bank recently critiqued Poland for its failure to understand the value of second-chance entrepreneurs as manifested in its particularly onerous liquidation procedures (Devictor 2013).

The present volume is a comprehensive compilation on the various aspects of the phenomenon of business failure, written by European authors.

Joanna Markiewicz and Leszek Gracz

Chapter 1

FROM LOSERS TO HEROES: HOW TO CHANGE THE PERCEPTION OF BUSINESS FAILURE AND RECOGNIZE ITS VALUE FOR THE ECONOMY

Joanna Markiewicz and Leszek Gracz

Abstract

This chapter sets out to explore the issue of the perception of business failure from the perspective of institutional theory. The statistics show that only 50 percent of businesses survive 5 years after they were created (Credireform 2002–06). Even though business deaths are normal for dynamic economic processes, the perception of failure is negative, especially on the European continent. While in the United States it is worthwhile, during a job interview, to admit to failure in business as it increases the value of potential employee, Europeans would rather remain silent about any lack of success in business. What can bring about a change related to a negative perception of business failure? To answer this question, institutional theory is used in the present study, especially the model of phases of institutional change. The chapter presents theoretical considerations as well as empirical evidence based on the research conducted during the realization of the Value of Failure project and in-depth interviews with entrepreneurs. As numerous scholars have shown that business failure is good for the economy and for society overall—due to the release of knowledge and resources from defunct businesses—the changed perception of failure will have a positive impact on the economy. The findings of the research show that lack of discussion about business failure in social life is one of the obstacles to recognizing its value. Media hype, engaging universities, business advisors and regional and local authorities in such discourses could be first steps in destabilization negative approaches.

Introduction

As the chapter investigates how to change the perception of business failure, the use of institutional theory, especially institutional change, seems to be a reasonable approach. Associated with incompetence and often hidden, such an approach to business failure does not encourage starting over. Greenwood's (Greenwood et al. 2002) theoretical concept of the process of institutional change is used in the study to propose change in the perception of business failure which, in fact, which, in fact, increased the knowledge and experience of entrepreneurs.

There is considerable business churn in the European Union and in the world. Many new enterprises are born and many vanish from the market. In the United States more than 80 percent of new firms end up failing, and about 10 percent of all American companies fold each year (DeGroat 2006). In the EU, between 2009 and 2011, an average of 200,000 firms went bankrupt annually. About one-quarter of those bankruptcies have a cross-border element, usually affecting more than one country. About 50 percent of all new businesses do not survive the first five years of their life. Every year, an estimated 1.7 million jobs are lost because of insolvencies.[1] Even though business failure seems to be a natural and common phenomenon, the overall perception of failure in Europe is negative, which in turn decreases both the number of new enterprises and restarted enterprises.

An interesting approach to business failure was undertaken within the project "Value of Failure,"[2] which was funded with support from the European Commission. The project's attempt to deal with the problem of the negative perception of business failure and its consequences included creating three regional "Second Chance Entrepreneurs Alliances." This strategy involved bringing together stakeholders in enterprise education and economic development—universities and colleges, Vocational Education and Training (VET) providers, enterprise development agencies, local governments, banks and chambers of commerce—to jointly contribute to sustainable cultural and institutional change regarding business failures. Having combined a group of various important stakeholders on a regional level, it was possible to implement a qualitative research method. The obvious choice was the focus group interview method, since there were both a well-established research sample and the necessary equipment in the Service Inter-Lab (the research center of Faculty of Management and Economics of Services of Poland's University of

---

1   Communication from the Commission to the European Parliament, the Council and the European Economic and Social Committee; "A new European approach to business failure and insolvency" /* COM/2012/0742 final */.
2   www.valueoffailure.com

Szczecin). The limitation of the method, as commonly agreed in the literature, is that, "while focus groups are an important preliminary step in exploring a subject, the results lack projectability to the larger population and should be treated cautiously" (Kotler, 2003). The next step after the focus group was individual in-depth interviews with chosen members of the Alliance, especially the second-chance entrepreneurs. This chapter studies the two approaches, presenting the findings on qualitative research of various stakeholders in Szczecin's region on changing the perception of business failure and recognizing its value for the economy.

Business Failure through the Lens of Institutional Theory

Institutional theory—theoretical bases

The attempt to explore how business failure is explained by institutional theory demands clarification of the main notions constituting the pillars of institutional theory, such as institutions, institutional change and institutional fields. A precursor of institutional theory, Thorstein Veblen (1899), assumed that institutions are made of collective habits or rules that create predictable regularities in behavior which shape people's activity. These considerations were developed by Douglas North (1990), who defines institutions as "the rules of the game in a society." These rules can be compared to constraints shaping human interactions.

The question arises as to how agents, who are embedded in such institutional frameworks (constraints), can introduce new institutions. Friedrich Hayek (1979) proposes the concept of a new path, which is followed by other agents. Similarly, institutions are followed by agents for whom it is easier to use already created paths. Another explanation was given by Paul DiMaggio (1988), who coined the term *institutional entrepreneurship*. According to this concept, there are individuals who are able to introduce institutions, and they act deliberately to achieve changes that have sufficient resources. Such an ability of actors to escape from institutional constraints (Rao 1998; Beckert 1999) is the opposite of the approach that assumes institutional change is the result of multiple institutional pressures that overlap and lead to contradictions (Seo and Creed 2002). Julie Battilana (2004) refers to this approach, arguing that institutional change is possible thanks to an institutional environment that encompasses multiple organizational fields. William Richard Scott and Douglas McAdam (2005) compare the institutional field to the concept of an "arena—system of actors, actions, and relations—whose participants take one another into account as they carry out interrelated activities." Using institutional fields, Battilana explains "the paradox of embedded agency." The agency of actors is triggered by the interference of institutional structures. Both internal tensions between different institutions in the field, as well as the transfer of schemas between different fields foster new institutional initiatives. Based on the assumption that institutional fields are not stable, Greenwood (Greenwood et al. 2002) made an attempt to illustrate the process of institutional change, proposing the following stages:

1. Precipitating jolts (destabilization);
2. Deinstitutionalization (disturbance in institutions);
3. Preinstitutionalization (introduction of innovation);
4. Theorization (assessment);
5. Diffusion (the spread of a new institution);
6. Reinstitutionalization (full institutionalization).

This concept is a pillar of further theoretical and empirical considerations, as this chapter aims to answer the question: What can bring about institutional change related to a negative perception of business failure? This means that the study should give insights on potential jolts, deinstitutionalization and preinstitutionalization, which can trigger the introduction of a new attitude toward business failure.

Approach to business failure

The theoretical aspect should also focus on an understanding of the business failure. Business failure is often called "exit," "death," "bankruptcy," "closure" or "liquidation." Nevertheless, some scholars emphasize that exit cannot always be used alternatively with failure (Coad 2014, Jenkins 2016). There is a distinction between the exit in which entrepreneurs are forced to abandon their firms because of insolvency and in which entrepreneurs close their businesses because they do not provide expected return on investment. Therefore, Alex Coad (2014) argues for the use of the term *business death*, which is appropriate to describe a business's exit in contrast to failure which, for example, can be understood as an unsuccessful acquisition of business, which can be continued. The difference between business survival and business death as defined by Coad (2014) is presented in Figure 1.1.

In this chapter we focus on failure connected with voluntary or involuntary death, according to Coad's analysis. Nevertheless, we argue that the term *death* can accentuate the pejorative perception of failure. Death in a biological sense is an irreversible phenomenon, which could suggest that entrepreneurs who have failed could not be reborn as entrepreneurs. Although Coad posits that

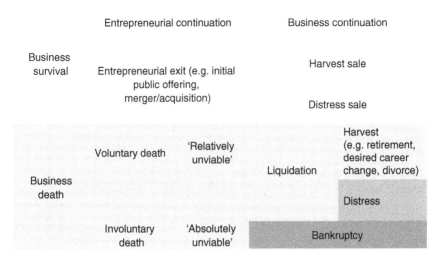

Figure 1.1 Analyzing business outcomes: A conceptual diagram.
Source: Coad, 2014.

the word *failure* implies that the firm's entire existence was a meaningless waste of time (Coad 2014, 727), we argue that failure often should be perceived as a state that can be improved.

Linking business failure with institutions, and taking into account the experience from the Value of Failure project, we observe that any lack of success in business is negatively perceived on the European continent. Even though learning from mistakes and from failure seems to be a sensible approach, entrepreneurs who have failed are omitted from any support as far as government or local prospects are concerned. Programs for enhancing economic development for the most part assume supporting start-ups using such tools as special loans, functioning of business incubators, etc. dedicated for start-ups only. Hence, entrepreneurs who have failed are expected not to start any business again. Political correctness tells us to promote and support those who have not been successful and enable them to start a new business. In reality, business failure is perceived more as *natural selection* in the economy, and entrepreneurs hide their failures.

Therefore, this study aims to provide valuable insights on possible initial stages of introducing institutional change regarding new perceptions of business failure. Two pieces of research conducted among different groups of stakeholders (entrepreneurs, scholars, local government representatives and business support organizations' representatives) ensure taking into account various institutional fields.

The Impact of Business Failure for the Economy

Numerous scholars have shown that business failure is good for the economy and society overall due to the release of knowledge and resources from defunct businesses (Ucbasaran et al. 2012). As stated, business churn in the EU causes many new enterprises to be born and many others to die and leave the market. According to Eurostat data, the general number of active enterprises in the EU is growing. The number of active enterprises consists of new and old companies. The dynamics of the birth of new enterprises varies in different countries. For instance, in the Netherlands and Portugal the numbers of new enterprises are decreasing, while in countries such as the Czech Republic and France the numbers are increasing. The dynamics of deaths of enterprises also varies in different countries. The comprehensive data, showing the net population of enterprises changes in the EU are presented in Table 1.1.

The general conclusions that can be derived from the numbers are that the market is very much alive; there are new enterprises emerging and some old enterprises die. However, the net numbers in some countries are negative, that is, more enterprises die than are born.

Entrepreneurs who have failed need an opportunity for a fresh start. Moreover, Europe needs to give them a second chance. Studies show that they learn from their mistakes, and that this leads to growth in GDP, employment and productivity (according to the EU Commission proposals for a Second Chance Policy). If Europe is to tap the full potential of its business self-starters, these entrepreneurs need both financial and moral support for their second ventures.

A recent study of the performances of Europe's fastest-growing companies shows that companies founded by restarters have higher turnover and employment growth than do companies run by entrepreneurs who have never failed (Rowe et al. 2002) According to Erik Stam et al. (2006) research shows that "second starters" are more successful and survive longer than do average start-ups; they grow faster and employ more workers. Thus, a failure in entrepreneurship should not result in a "life sentence" prohibiting any future entrepreneurial activity, but should be seen as an opportunity for learning and improving.

Business failure does not mean losing the entrepreneurial spirit. Research shows that a large majority of people whose businesses failed still had plans for new business projects (Stam and Schutjens 2006). Having already faced extreme challenges, many entrepreneurs who fail at the first hurdle are willing and able to learn from their mistakes. They may also have developed greater determination and a highly sensitive radar for danger, which will help them more effectively assess risks and opportunities.

Table 1.1 The net population of enterprise changes in EU (where applicable) in the years 2008–12.

GEO/TIME	2008	2009	2010	2011	2012
Belgium	10,662	4,857	10,033	14,192	15,194
Bulgaria	13,845	31,969	11,240	–4,122	3,387
Czech Republic	–36,855	25,390	24,060	–1,231	1,655
Denmark		–5,729	–405	3,378	–3,680
Germany (until 1990 former territory of the FRG)	274,803	–17,098	4,953	3,455	–3,876
Estonia	3,723	–3,392	729	2,503	1,691
Ireland	–7,576	–9,153	–4,879	–6,229	2,058
Spain	–65,175	–75,906	–38,534	–46,180	–48,777
France	52,565	153,095	174,357	134,766	136,891
Croatia					–6,151
Italy	2,868	45,854	7,077	–52,024	–40,855
Cyprus	522	–447	–1,734	–2,762	–2,997
Latvia	–18	1,194	4785	6,114	9,951
Lithuania	–12,673	–8,199	5,046	9,224	31,086
Luxembourg	564	512	567	603	593
Hungary	–3,779	–2,642	–6,038	–29,707	–36,298
Malta			1,355	–2,640	263
Netherlands	50,889	49,722	14,099	41,676	–8,920
Austria	2,933	–214	–666	–1,770	–272
Poland	76,072	38,717	63,268	3,668	229,174
Portugal	–7549	–37468	–33381	–50,706	–51,062
Romania	22,021	–55,820	–51,874	31162	57253
Slovenia	5,755	4,667	2,250	2,393	2,290
Slovakia	14,289	20,939	22,472	–6,531	9,792
Finland	6,771	1,633	3,954		
Sweden	7,746	5,945	10,102	21,311	–4,135
United Kingdom	26,615	–85,680	–13,405	29,750	16,630
Norway	7,493	6,445	4,578	7,971	7,411
Switzerland					
Turkey		685	–338,277	717,573	

Note: The numbers were calculated as the number of births of enterprises minus the number of deaths of enterprises.

Source: Authors' elaboration based on Eurostat data, 2014.

Method

Two phases of research

Beaver and Jennings note that in attempting to understand business failure, business owners are extremely unwilling to report the true reasons for the problems, especially if the reasons are personal limitations (Beaver and Jennings 2005). They further argue that the use of surveys drives dissonant responses. Therefore, in this study the qualitative approach has been undertaken, seeking to create safe conditions for open discussion on this sensitive approach. Two levels of privacy were established:

* general discussion on the perception of failure and ways of dealing with the issue;
* discussion on the personal experience of individuals who suffered business failure.

In cases of a general discussion, the focus group interview method was chosen. For personal experience, individual in-depth interviews were applied.

In order to explore the data collected through the focus group interview and in-depth interviews, discourse analysis was employed in this study. To explain the idea of discourse analysis, it is worthwhile to see du Gay (2000), who argues that discourse analysis "is a group of statements that provide a way of talking about and acting upon a particular object. When statements about an object or topic are made from within a certain discourse, that discourse makes it possible to construct that object in a particular way" (du Gay 2000, 67). The broad understanding of discourse analysis makes this term vague, as some academics relate it with historical studies and others with critical analysis. I assume that discourse analysis contributes to cognizance of the role of institutions that shape the relations between social actors. These relations are revealed in meanings and understandings that dominate in social life. To prove this approach, we refer to Cynthia Hardy and Nelson Phillips's (1999) arguments that depict discourse "as a system of texts that bridges an object into being [...] Discourse is therefore the foundation of the process of social construction upon which social reality depends" (Hardy and Phillips 1999, 2).

Focus Group Interview

Focus groups are defined in the literature as either "in-depth group interviews employing relatively homogenous groups to provide information around topics specified by the researchers" or "carefully planned discussion[s] designed to obtain perceptions on a defined environment" (Smithson 2000). The difference between these two approaches is concentration on discussion or interview (which means asking questions and receiving answers). The approach used by the chair of Services Marketing at the University of Szczecin is to combine the interview with discussion, creating the "controlled group discussion," which benefits from both group interaction processes, and leading the process by a moderator asking proper questions.

The focus group interviews with selected members of the Second Chance Entrepreneurs Alliance were conducted in the facility of the Service Inter-Lab (the research center of Faculty of Management and Economics of Services at the University of Szczecin). The focus group took place in February 2015. The research group included entrepreneurs, scholars, local government representatives and business support organizations representatives. The fields of expertise of participants were finance, banking, communication and psychology, economics, neuro-economics and administration. The group consisted of 12 persons. The moderator was Leszek Gracz, chair of Services Marketing. The agenda of the discussion was:

- What do they think of business failure? What is their perception of business failure?
- Is there anything special about Szczecin's region with regard to business failure?
- Since there is a negative perception of business failure, what can be the actual benefit for second-chance entrepreneurs?
- Who (both people and institutions) should be involved in the actions concerning support of second-chance entrepreneurs?

The findings were elaborated in accordance with the assumptions of the abovementioned discourse analysis. The transcript of the focus group was translated into English and then, in accordance with the text and moderator notes, key issues were established, constituting the basis for general findings.

Focus Group Interviews—Findings

Concerning the perception of business failure, all participants were convinced that it is a serious issue, especially in Europe. One participant, a representative of local self-government, shared the experience of an economic mission by Polish entrepreneurs to Silicon Valley in the United States, in 2014. What was shocking for these entrepreneurs was the "cult of failure." American entrepreneurs who went bankrupt perceived it as something to be proud about. During so-called phishing (presenting a business idea for potential investors—venture capital) there were questions like "How many times have you been bankrupted? Which attempt at business was that?" And the more failures one had in the past, the better one's chances for finding potential investors. It shows the difference between how failure is perceived in Europe and in the United States.

Another important aspect of failure has its roots in cognitive theory. During a discussion initiated by a philosophy professor (academic point of view) all the participants learned there are actually no positive words in the Polish language for explaining the phenomenon of failure. All words that are synonymous have wrong connotations. This makes it difficult to speak about failure without negative connotations.

According to representatives of Business Environment Institutions (BEI) and entrepreneurs, the typical perception of the failed entrepreneur in Poland is based on two common characterizations: a failed entrepreneur is either a loser or someone who committed fraud. According to the research, these are of course wrong assumptions, yet they are deeply stuck in the minds of Poles. The participants are convinced this approach is a broadly accepted in Poland, and there are no distinctive differences in Szczecin's region.

Another aspect raised by participants is that, from the academic point of view, fear of failure is actually a strong factor that demotivates students from starting their own enterprises; examples were as follows:

- The students fear the potential troubles they may face when something goes wrong with their business;
- The social thread of failure is strong, as one participant said she heard from a student: "I could start a business, but how to tell my friends on Facebook if I failed in business?"
- Many students think that failure is often because of bureaucracy; they do not want to start their own business because they fear all the procedures and bureaucracy that may lead them to failure.

Having agreed that failure is in fact something good, the focus group participants began to explore possible solutions to the current situation. Ideas were as follows:

1. Scholars:
   - we should teach the students about failure, the value of failure and how to recover from failure;
   - we should use the resources we have as higher education institutions, especially the carrier offices.

2. Business support organization representatives:
   - the organizations involved in an economic aspect of society, such as associations, chambers and so forth, should be aware of the phenomenon and actively take part in promoting the value of failure;

- there should be some lobbying for government and self-government institutions to elaborate state or regional programs dedicated to the failed entrepreneurs;
- there is a need for administrative actions concerning the issues; tax offices, social insurance and employment offices should be especially aware of the program;
- there is a growing trend toward personal advice in business; there are more and more coaches and personal trainers who work closely with entrepreneurs and should be also targeted by the program.

3. Entrepreneurs:
   - people who have failed in business probably are not willing to share their experience; perhaps a reward for a restarter, organized by a prestigious entity, would help in changing that;
   - the change in how failed entrepreneurs are perceived should also take place in the mass media, where failed entrepreneurs could be presented as valuable for society and the economy;
   - there is a common perception that business failure is treated as a threat by banks during the credit-application process. Therefore, many people with experience and good business plans cannot receive bank credit. They have to conceal their previous bankruptcy.

4. Local government representatives:
   - the policy for second-chance entrepreneurs is very important; however, it should be carefully noted that potential help is given to "honest failures" but not to potential frauds;
   - there is a lack of EU programs aimed at failed entrepreneurs. All the EU programs are targeted at special groups, mostly young and elderly people. There are hardly any programs for middle-age persons.

The general conclusion from the focus group interview confirms the importance of failed entrepreneurs for the economy and the need of bringing second-chance entrepreneurs back into the market. Various points of view (the perspective of entrepreneurs, scholars, local government representatives and business support organizations representatives) result, with several ideas on changing the perception of failed entrepreneurs from losers to heroes.

In-Depth Interviews

The selection of entrepreneurs for in-depth interviews was based on their experience of failure (business death according to Coad). The group of

Table 1.2 The characteristics of entrepreneurs included in the research.

Id.	Current industry	Previous industry
1e.	Trade	Construction
2e.	Consulting	Trade
3e.	Construction	Consulting
4e.	Advertising	Advertising
5e.	Consulting	Advertising
6e.	Consulting	Consulting

Source: Authors' own research.

entrepreneurs meeting such criteria was selected thanks to collaboration with the Northern Chamber of Commerce in Szczecin. The interviewees were recruited from the owners of firms and, therefore, CEOs and managers were interviewed. Altogether, six entrepreneurs were interviewed. Joanna Markiewicz conducted these discussions in May–June 2016. Information about the entrepreneurs who took part in the research is presented in Table 1.2

The work on data was in accordance with the assumptions of discourse analysis. After the in-depth interviews were transcribed,[3] the key phrases were found in the text. After the revision key phrases were grouped into categories. These stages allowed the emergence of theoretical dimensions.

In-Depth Interviews—Findings

All interviewees admitted that their business failures constituted the best lesson in their business lives. Although this lesson was rather traumatic experience, the knowledge gained was used in their current businesses. The value of knowledge was emphasized by every participant in the interviews. For example, interviewee 2e said, "I've got a master's degree in economics. When I was starting my business, I thought I knew everything. And I was sure that I would be successful in business. I believed too much in my intuition. I was sure that my products would take over the greater part of the market. Now I know how wrong I was and how carefully one has to analyze the market demand. I'm not in trade any more. But, providing consulting services, I use the lesson from my failure very often. It helps (laugh)." Interviewee 6e confirmed the importance of knowledge: "I use my experience of failure as a case study while working with my clients. I think that this experience makes me more credible to my clients, who are entrepreneurs and who prefer to learn

---

3   The author translated the transcripts from Polish into English.

from somebody [else's] mistakes." But 6e confessed that when he went bankrupt, he did not want to tell his family: "It was hard [Silence]. What could I say? That I devoted my time and money to start the firm and then failed after a few months? I think my parents still don't know the whole truth. They know that I had some financial problems, and I changed the profile of my business." Interviewee 1e said: "You'd better not say that you experienced bankruptcy. Other entrepreneurs would give [you] to understand that business is not the best occupation for you. I easily talk about my failure now, when xxx (1e's firm) is successful. Before, I would rather keep it to myself." The above-mentioned statements prove that shame, secrecy and intention of hiding the fact of failure dominated the discourse.

What is more, grief and bitterness that business failure is not properly recognized, and thus is underestimated, intertwined in the opinions of the majority of interviewed entrepreneurs. Interviewee 5e said, "I can't understand why there is such glorification of start-ups. I realize that new companies are important for the economy, but when I analyze the programs providing financial help for them I think it's a waste of money. I provide consulting services, so I know various programs. Can you imagine that young people starting their businesses might get grants, which are really good money, buy a computer, apps, and so forth, and act as a sole proprietor for at best least a year and that's it? Ninety percent of them would not exist after this time! Why is there no financial help for those who failed and want to restart their business? I bet more than a half of such firms would survive on the market." Interviewee 4e also referred to the support from the state: "When I had to close my business, I couldn't count on any help. Is there any help for bankrupts? I don't think so. Awareness, that's a key word. People do not realize what experience such an entrepreneur has, with employees, finance, market. In my opinion, such people should be encouraged to start a business again."

Interviewee 3e raised another issue connected with business failure—education. "When I was an academic lecturer, I taught management. I realized there is very little attention paid to the topic of business failure. Of course, topics like reasons for failure, mistakes that should be avoided, and so forth, but no focus on the restart of a business."

The attitude of young people toward business failure was mentioned by 4e. He expressed his opinion about students and young people entering the real business world: "The Y generation aren't fighters. They prefer to realize their passions, [but] business is not so important for them. We don't have many subjects at schools and universities that would develop creativity and the business approach. Besides, our society has a negative perception of business failure, which additionally is discouraging for entrepreneurs to restart their business."

The discourse revealed the attitude toward entrepreneurs who experienced business failure. Feelings of a shame and attempts to hide the fact of failure indicate that such entrepreneurs are marginalized. Such a degrading experience implies other consequences, like avoiding the topic in public life (policy, support programs, education). What is more, lack of interest in knowledge deriving from failure can be observed. Such conclusions from this part of the research can set in motion the following proposals leading to institutional change, according to the Greenwood et al. model:

1. Public consultation (also among business) about support for second-chance entrepreneurs as destabilization of existing institutions.
2. Introducing support for second-chance entrepreneurs in regional/local policies as a disturbance in institutions.
3. Launching programs offering various forms of support for second-chance entrepreneurs (introduction of innovation).

Public consultation on support for second-chance entrepreneurs would increase the awareness of business failure among various group of actors. Including support for second-chance entrepreneurs would mean the recognition of the importance of the knowledge and potential of second-chance entrepreneurs. Offering real help for such people would indicate that the experience of business failure is valuable and that it is worth helping them to start their businesses again.

Conclusion

Two phases of the qualitative research provided valuable insights into potential actions aiming at commencing institutional change in the perception of business failure. Despite the differences between the research methods and the group of participants (different institutional fields), one can indicate a common denominator in the findings, and in this way propose final conclusions concerning possible ways of changing the perception of business failure.

The findings show that business failure is treated as a "forbidden issue." Even though business death is natural for the economy, closures and bankruptcies are perceived as misfortune and disaster. Entrepreneurs who have failed are considered losers who cannot succeed in business. Therefore, entrepreneurs who have experienced failure usually do not reveal that part of their business history. Besides, a lack of awareness about the knowledge and value of experience coming from failure can be observed. In order to commence

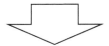

Media hype about business failure; business advisors, universities and vocational education training institutions discuss business failure; public consultation about support for second-chance entrepreneurs

Destabilization of existing institution

Support for second-chance entrepreneurs in regional/local policies; business failure in educational programmes

Disturbance in institution

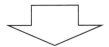

Programmes offering various forms of support for second-chance entrepreneurs; reward for successful restarters

Introduction of innovation

Figure 1.2 Proposal of actions aiming at institutional change in the perception of business failure.
Source: Based on Greenwood et al.'s (2002) model of institutional change.

the change in perception that is reflected in the changes at institutions, following the phases in the institutional change process indicated by Greenwood et al. (2002) we propose the actions seen in Figure 1.2.

The presented issue is complex and requires considerable time to achieve actual results. Changes in perception and attitudes have to do with, among other things, beliefs, feelings and behavior. Change is possible, however, and many EU programs have proved to have an actual impact. It is now time to change the perception of failed entrepreneurs: from losers to heroes.

References

Battilana, Julie (2004). "Foundations for a Theory of Institutional Entrepreneurship: Solving the paradox of embedded agency," *Faculty and Research*, INSEAD, 2004/61/OB.

Beaver, Graham and Jennings, Peter (2005). "Competitive advantage and entrepreneurial power: The dark side of entrepreneurship." *Journal of Small Business and Enterprise Development* 12(1): 9–23.

Beckert, Jens (1999). "Agency, entrepreneurs, and institutional change: The role of strategic choice and institutionalized practices." *Organization Studies* 20(5): 777–99.

Coad, Alexander. (2014). "Death is not a success: Reflections on business exit." *International Small Business Journal* 32(7): 721–32.

DeGroat, Bernard. (2012). "Business failures are good for the economy: A new European approach to business failure and insolvency." http://ns.umich.edu/new/releases/478

DiMaggio, Paul Joseph (1998). "Interest and agency in institutional theory." In: Lynne G. Zucker (Ed.). *Institutional Patterns and Organizations: Culture and Environment* (3–22). Cambridge, MA: Ballinger Publishing Co.

Du Gay, Paul (2000) "Markets and meaning: Re-imagining organizational life." In Schultz, Majken, Hatch, Mary Jo and Larsen, Mogens Holten (Eds.). *The Expressive Organization: Linking Identity, Reputation, and the Corporate Brand*. Oxford: Oxford University Press.

European Commission (2012). "A new European approach to business failure and insolvency." http://ec.europa.eu/justice/civil/files/insolvency-comm_en.pdf

Greenwood, Royston, Suddaby, Roy and Hinings, C. R. (2002). "Theorizing change: The role of professional associations in the transformation of institutional fields." *Academy of Management Journal* 45(1): 58–80.

Hardy, Cynthia and Phillips, Nelson (1999). "No Joking Matter: Discursive Struggle in the Canadian Refugee System." *Organization Studies* 20: 1–24.

Hayek, Friedrich (1979). "*The Counter-Revolution of Science: Studies on the Abuse of Reason.*" 2nd edn. Indianapolis: Liberty Press.

Jenkins, Anna and McKelvie, Alexander (2016). "What is entrepreneurial failure? Implications for future research." *International Small Business Journal* 34(2): 176–88.

Kotler, Philip (2003). *Marketing Insights from A to Z* (116). John Wiley and Sons.

McAdam, Doug and Scott, W. Richard (2005). "Organizations and movements." In Gerald F. Davis, Doug McAdam, W. Richard Scott, Mayer N. Zald (Eds.). *Social Movements and Organization Theory* (4–41). New York: Cambridge University Press.

North, Douglass Cecil (1990). *Institutions, Institutional Change and Economic Performance.* New York: Cambridge University Press.

Rao, Hayagreeva (1998). "Caveat emptor: The construction of non-profit consumer watchdog organizations." *American Journal of Sociology* 103(4): 912–61.

Rowe, Nicola, Riedler, Susanne and Odenstein, Holger (2002). *Setting the Phoenix Free: A Report on Entrepreneurial Restarters.* The Boston Consulting Group.

Seo, Myeong-Gu and Creed, W. E. Douglas (2002). "Institutional contradictions, praxis, and institutional change: A dialectical perspective." *Academy of Management Review* 27: 222–47.

Smithson, Janet (2000). Using and analysing focus groups: Limitations and possibilities. *International Journal of Social Research Methodology* 3(2): 104.

Stam, Erik, Audretsch, David B. and Meijaard, Joris (2006). "Renascent Entrepreneurship." Erasmus Research Institute of Management.

Stam, Erik and Shutjens, Veronique (2006). "Starting anew: Entrepreneurial intentions and realizations subsequent to business closure." Series: Papers on Entrepreneurship,

Growth and Public Policy, Max Planck Institute of Economics, Entrepreneurship, Growth and Public Policy Group. Jena.

Ucbasaran, Deniz, Shepherd, Dean A., Lockett, Andy and Lyon, John (2012). "Life after Business Failure: The Process and Consequences of Business Failure for Entrepreneurs," Warwick Business School, Working Paper no. 117, 1.

Veblen, Thorstein (1899). *The Theory of the Leisure Class*. New York: Penguin Books.

Chapter 2

ECONOMIC FAILURE IN THE PROCESS OF SMALL BUSINESS GROWTH IN THE CONTEXT OF THE SHADOW ECONOMY

Edward Stawasz and Jarosław Ropęga

Abstract

This chapter discusses economic failure in the process of small business growth, using the example of Polish companies operating in the *shadow economy*. The discussion covers internal and external barriers contributing to economic failure in the process of company growth. The presence of companies in the shadow economy influences their operation and consequently the process of their growth. On the one hand, it stimulates the efficiency of businesses and, on the other, it boosts the risk of failure due to possible overestimated investment profitability, the confidential nature of internal activity in a company and problems in contacts with the surroundings. Such a risk is increasing with the increase of the shadow economy's financing of the company's growth.

Introduction

Small businesses have specific market, finance, location, organization and technology features that define their operational and strategic behavior, which are different than in large companies. Due to those features a small business is not merely a downscaled large company (Storey 1994). Differences in companies of various scale can be seen when it comes to development as well. Contrary to large companies, the majority of small businesses are in the early stages of their operations and only some of them succeed and grow to become a larger, stable and expandable company. With the growth of the scale of business, a company faces new problems and challenges in terms of management, finance and technology, and they contribute to various barriers and risk factors. According to the literature, we observe concentration of attention interchangeably on internal and external barriers and factors causing economic failure in the process of company growth (Ropęga and Stawasz 2014; Blackburn et al. 2013; Wiklund et al. 2009; Garnsey et al. 2006). One of the less examined factors is the share of companies in the shadow economy and the impact of the latter on the growth of small businesses (Stawasz and Głodek 2009; Caca 2010).

Shadow economy activity complements the legal sphere of business limited to certain areas only. In 2010–15, the scale of the shadow economy was about 19.7–18.5 percent of businesses in EU member states, whereas in Poland it was 23–24 percent (Schneider 2015). Retail, construction and property and business services have the largest influence on the scale of the shadow economy. Considering its scale, research of the phenomenon so far has been less intensive and covers mainly the shadow economy and pathological behavior in the economy, whereas the research concentrates less on examining of the mechanism and behavior of companies in the shadow economy with the use of model approaches, typical for today's economics (Schneider and Enste 2000). The impact of the shadow economy on the operation of companies seems to be diverse when we analyze the scale, location and links between companies and their environments (Hudson et al. 2012; Schneider et al. 2015). It seems that this issue should be taken into consideration by the economic policy and management practice (Caca 2010; Williams 2007).

The main advantage for businesses operating in the shadow economy, usually small to medium-sized enterprises (SMEs), is the possibility of avoiding the obligation to pay taxes and other statutory dues, which also reduces time spent on formalities related to running a business (e.g., business registration, applying for permits and licenses for specific production, export permits, registration of property to obtain crediting and so forth.). In specific circumstances, the shadow economy helps in gaining market and entrepreneurial experience, and consequently in promoting quick growth (Stawasz and Głodek 2009).

Goal and Scope of the Chapter

Various internal and external barriers, including lack of knowledge on management's part, influence different areas of company activity and may hamper growth. In a small company, to adopt a growth strategy an entrepreneur needs to understand risks and barriers in resources and competences and the necessity to analyze them and undertake required steps. While counteracting the above growth barriers, small businesses decide to move to the shadow economy to improve the efficiency of their investment, on the one hand. On the

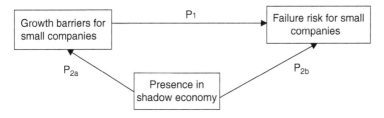

Figure 2.1 Proposed influence model.
Source: Authors' study.

other hand, such a decision involves additional challenges for mangers and, consequently, may contribute to their later failure.

The goals of the chapter is to present barriers and risk factors determining the growth of Polish small businesses in the economy under transformation, and an attempt to assess the significance of the shadow economy as a factor influencing barriers to growth and economic failure. A model of those relations is presented in Figure 2.1. The chapter includes three proposals:

- Proposal P_1 Growth barriers for small businesses increase the risk of failure in the process of their growth; whereas the weakening of a barrier reduces the risk of failure, and the larger the scale of a company, the larger the influence.
- Proposal P_{2a} Operation of a small business in the shadow economy may reduce growth barriers for companies, and the larger the operation in the shadow economy the larger the influence.
- Proposal P_{2b} The operation of small businesses in the shadow economy may increase the risk of company failure.

The chapter examines foreign and domestic literature on growth barriers for small businesses and business risk related to those barriers. The description of the shadow economy and determining of factors stimulating the development and reducing barriers and mitigating risks is based on the study of literature, as well as on empirical analyses of the operation of the Polish SME sector. The chapter uses findings of research by the authors covering 131 Polish SMEs in 2007–08, research funded by the Scientific Research Committee on Management of SMEs Growth in the Context of the Shadow Economy.

Barriers for SMEs' Growth

Currently, companies operate in a rapidly changing environment, and the prevailing features of the economy are uncertainty and volatility. That uncertainty for small businesses is higher than for large ones due to reduced impact on their environments as well as weakness of internal management systems. Rapid technological, economic and social changes are the main source of uncertainty for companies that produce a high risk of crisis. High uncertainty for small businesses exposes companies to a high risk of failure, in particular in the case of new ones. According to domestic and foreign statistics, the risk of failure in business is high during the first five years of operation. According to Eurostat, only 44 percent of businesses have five years of survival (*Business* 2016).

SME is a sector showing significant heterogeneity. The sector is very diverse from the point of view of motivation and business goals and contacts with the environment depending on the form and nature of ownership, geographic location and scope of business, development stage and organizational and legal form, and so forth. This translates into a number of development opportunities for those companies. It is unquestioned that growth and development are a precondition for the survival of small businesses. Once they move to another stage of development, the companies increase their scale of operation, while investing in new technologies and new products, and expanding production capacity and entering new markets, international markets included. Changes related to that growth of businesses are followed by changes in all business areas.

The diversity of development behavior among SMEs is the result of various factors—factors that show complex mutual links and weight for the operation of companies. Although it is possible to identify key growth factors for various types of companies, it is extremely difficult to determine a cohesive growth model that enables predicting their growth and development (Smallbone, Leigh and North 1995; Levie and Lichtenstein 2010). Literature provides a number of growth and development concepts and several approaches to the issue, such as: development as integration of the strategy and structure (Chandler 1962; O'Farrell and Hitchins 2002), growth and development as evolution and revolution (Greiner 1972), changes of prevailing functions (Adizes 2004), internal and external growth (Bleicher 1991), integrated approach based on growth and development factors (Storey 1994; Davidsson. Achtenhagen and Naldi 2010; Wiklund 1998; Quinn and Cameron 1983, Levie and Lichtenstein 2010), and growth and development of small and medium-sized businesses (Churchill and Lewis 1983). Many of those concepts are based on distinguishing a number of stages organizations go through during their growth and development. As the company moves from lower to upper phases of development, new problems appear in specific business areas and the weight of particular factors determining its growth changes. For instance, in SMEs at the early stage factors related to the owner, such as motivation, capacity and managerial and strategic skills are decisive as regards operation and success or failure. At further stages, those factors give in to the delegation of responsibilities and strategic skills (Churchill and Lewis 1983).

Small companies have the possibility of choosing their development paths, depending on their internal potential and opportunities created by their environment. Frequently, the specific nature of their management determines development strategies. They operated under a shortage of resources, in particular material and financial resources, and the owner plays a dominating role in their organization system. We can distinguish two categories of SMEs depending on their approach to development challenges (Bullock et al. 2004; Majumdar 2008; Katz and Greek 2007):

- Companies oriented on development applying a strategic approach focused on spotting and using opportunities, and having ambitious and visionary owners. They are entrepreneurial and fast growing, often in the area of high-tech.
- Companies with poor development orientation, focused on short-term goals, and quick effects utilized by their owners. Frequently, this group includes income substitution companies, self-employed lifestyle businesses and small family-owned firms, for example, in retail. This group includes companies concentrated on consumption and partially operating in the shadow economy.

Rapid growth of the first group depends on the owner who might be open to changes, to perceive growth as success, capable of taking risks and resorting to external resources. Entrepreneurs from the second group promote growth when it is necessary: they focus on survival, avoid risk and are not willing to give up control over the company.

The focus on growth depends on a number of factors. Their comprehensive examination can be found in integrated growth models. David Storey (Storey 1994) provides a list of 35 growth factors in three categories: entrepreneur, company and management and strategy, whereas Per Davidsson (Davidsson 1991) specifies factors related to the owner, his or her needs related to the growth of the company and environment-based factors, such as occasions and opportunities. In the model developed by J. Robert Baum et al. (Baum, Locke and Smith 2001) particular factors interact leading to success and growth of the company. Factors in this model include: entrepreneur qualities and skills, sector-related and technical skills, motivation, competitive strategies and the environment. The model by Johan Wiklund et al. (Wiklund, Patzelt and Shepherd 2009) takes into consideration a combination of internal and external factors determining the growth of SMEs: entrepreneurial orientation, outside conditions, resources and the attitude of the owner to development.

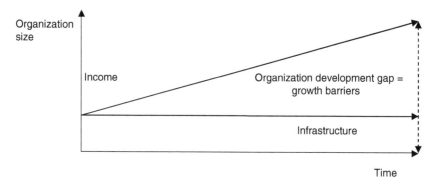

Figure 2.2 Organization development gap.
Source: Flamholtz and Randle 2007, 5.

A number of studies on growth and development in small businesses distinguish between internal and external factors (Davidsson et al. 2010; Gupta et al. 2013). Those factors can be constructive and destructive as regards the development of a company. Destructive factors, in other words growth barriers, make the development of a company more difficult and may lead to major interruptions in its operation and, in extreme cases (when no remedial action is taken), to the collapse of a company.

External growth barriers for SMEs are chiefly related to institutional factors, such as taxation, labor law, regulations, political stability and status of the economy. An important barrier hampering growth of small businesses is reduced access to external sources of funding. Internal barriers are usually associated with weaknesses of companies and may include the entrepreneur, strategies, management style and resources available.

Growth barriers appear when the organizational development starts lagging behind business growth (Figure 2.2). If a company fails to develop its operational and management systems, structure and processes supporting growth, it may not be able to move to another development phase.

Growth barriers referred to by a number of authors—which are the most important from the point of view of small businesses—include those related to management and finance.

In most instances, barriers related to inefficient management of small businesses are determined by the entrepreneur. Key decisions regarding the company are usually made by one person—the owner. His or her personality traits and attitudes determine management and the probability of success or failure. John Argenti (Argenti 1976) refers to the owner being a key factor determining success or failure of the company and describes those factors as "innate" flaws of a company. The experience and skills of the owner determine the quality of management in the company. Barriers in management include the following (Bartlett and Bukovic 2001; Storey 1994):

- Low level of knowledge and skills (insufficient skills and competences, as well as low learning capability);
- Mistakes in development strategy;
- Lack of will to delegate; and
- Failure to concentrate on operation.

The management process in micro and small businesses, which is intuitive and focused on solving current issues, does not create favorable conditions for the development of those companies. In terms of management, a problem for micro and small businesses is also access to information and its analysis, in particular lack of time for in-depth analysis of information, misinterpretation of signals and limited financial resources. These problems result from information barriers faced by small companies in their operations (Ropega 2013):

- Information barriers as such—lack of information about a given issue, low quality of information available or incomplete information and information accessed too late.
- Psychological barriers—selective approach to information depending on individual preferences of the owner and overflow of information.
- Sociological barriers—autocratic management style prevailing in small businesses, social norms limiting and determining perception, assigning meaning and assessment of issues.
- Organizational barriers—poor organization of information, information noise; and
- Economic barriers—shortage of funding to implement an information system.

Information barriers are a real limitation for creating competence in an entrepreneur and the organization. In practical terms, this results in recognized and unrecognized shortages of competences accompanied with the lack of the possibility to gain relevant information on, among others, available solutions or potential knowledge.

Management and information barriers, which have a major influence on the operation and growth of traditional, family-owned small businesses that are ways of earning a living for their owners. Those barriers may become factors contributing to failure of those companies. According to the literature, the majority of failures occur due to management errors (Argenti 1976; Slatter and Lovett 1999). Studies of bankruptcy in small businesses in the United

States (Bradley III 2000) confirm the above. According to such studies, some prevailing reasons for failure in small businesses include insufficient management skills, poor knowledge regarding the operation of the company and a shortage of capital.

Growth in small businesses requires change in the management system. The growing scale of business is followed by increased complexity of operations; simple structures and decision making powers are not enough to provide efficient management of growth. In order to introduce changes to the management system, it is necessary to overcome a certain psychological barrier, development threshold related to a transformation from intuitive to professional management (Katz and Green 2007).

Further barriers determining growth in small businesses are financial ones. Small businesses, in particular in the early stages of their development, are funded from the personal resources of the owner or the family, and they suffer from a permanent shortage of working capital. Growth necessitates changes in the capital structure and attracting external capital. However, a company is not always developed enough to be a credible client for financial institutions. Canadian studies (Baldwin et al. 1997) indicate three main mistakes in financial management that can be considered reasons for failure:

- Inability to manage working capital;
- Shortage of capital;
- Inappropriate capita structure.

The first factor is related to previously mentioned factors linked with the management skills of the entrepreneur. Two others are related to management mistakes (no financial control, too low an equity level, excessive indebtedness and also an aversion to taking credit and being subject of a control), as well as imperfections of the capital market (barriers to access capital established by financial institutions) and information barriers (shortage of information about various financing opportunities).

The operation of the company is based on resources and opportunities and the way opportunities are taken to implement and utilize resources (Amit and Schomaker 1993). While referring to the evolution theory by Richard R. Nelson and Sidney G. Winter (1982), Robert M. Grant (1991) defines opportunities as interacting routines, coordination between people and between people and other resources. The type, size and quality of resources available in an organization are crucial for overcoming limitations in creating routines, and it influences their standard. Interactions and relations between resources and capacity as well as strategic external factors determine strategic assets necessary to generate profit. From a resource-based view, for the company to establish its competitive advantage, such resources (Barney 1991) should be: valuable, rare, inimitable and non-substitutable. According to Jay Barney (1991; 2001), although all those criteria are important for survival in a competitive environment, the most important is the difficulty of copying or imitating resources by the competition. The unique nature of tangible resources is difficult to achieve (apart from some exceptions, they are commonly available), whereas unique combinations of intangible resources can strengthen the competitive position of a company. In the group of small and micro companies, the most valuable, rare and inimitable resources include informal privileged relations with the environment (Chandra, Styles and Wilkinson 2009). Such resources are considered the most useful to take advantage of opportunities and, apart from knowledge, to reduce risks. Other important, unique and valuable resources in small companies include attitudes and behavior of employees. More costly resources, such as technologies and IT systems, that are not indicated by small firms as valuable and original, confirm barriers in that area.

Successful growth and further operation of a small firm depend on reducing the negative impact of external and internal weaknesses. Information barriers in small businesses result in uncertainty in decision making, and the risk of failure may be impossible to estimate. Such risk appears before reasons for failure. Then, when the risk materializes, its effects may become one of the reasons for failure. For example, dependence of a firm on a single supplier or client is not by itself a reason for failure, but bankruptcy or breach of contract can seriously interrupt the activity of a firm and threaten its further existence. Owners of small businesses frequently point to low-risk awareness in their activity, the effects of which can be important for survival. The awareness of risk and protection against it become more important the smaller the scale of business activity. Small firms find it more difficult to deal with such risk than larger ones (Henschel 2008). On the one hand, failure to recognize risk may result in an inability to implement actions planned and, on the other, exaggeration and lack of knowledge about possibilities to exercise control may discourage promoting the development of a company.

Barriers in micro and small businesses related to management and competences may increase the probability of various types of risk in those organizations. It may happen in the case of internal risks that depend on a specific nature of a firm. For example, mistakes in management of capital increase the risk of losing liquidity, and inept management of personnel may result in more frequent fraud by employees or in their transfer to the competition. Risk of bankruptcy or termination of cooperation by a key client is much higher when an entrepreneur makes strategic mistakes regarding selecting suppliers or clients (Cf. Bartlet and Buković 2001).

The Influence of the Shadow Economy on the Operation and Growth of Small Businesses

According to Polish entrepreneurs, activity in the shadow economy is under-taken cautiously (Stawasz and Głodek 2009). The main advantage is the possibility to avoid taxes and other dues imposed by the state through a regulatory framework (Djankow et al. 2002). According to a number of studies, for 60 percent of businesses this activity enables reducing the shortage of capital. In certain circumstances, operating in the shadow economy (as expressed by one fourth of companies surveyed) enables gaining market and entrepreneurial experience. Therefore, operation in the shadow economy is determined by economic and development factors. To a certain extent customs in a given sector play their role in moving to the shadow economy (7% of companies surveyed).

The intention to get rich fast due to accumulation of funds by operating in the shadow economy has an impact on the operation of firms. Profits generated in the shadow economy may be spent for private consumption as well as investment in a company. The vast majority of entrepreneurs designate the shadow economy profit for their personal consumption.

Some companies, however, designate this type of profit to promoting investment and growth. It seems that a natural relation can be distinguished, namely: action taken to reduce shortages of capital by operation in the shadow economy aims at increasing a company's profit and, consequently, promoting growth. However, this is rare among entrepreneurs operating in the shadow economy due to poor growth tendency and their aversion to taking additional risk related to management of growth in the shadow economy and the need to improve their managerial competence.

Growth of a company in the shadow economy may result in extremely different assessments among external stakeholders, chiefly financial institutions, business partners and public authorities. Such assessments may influence the success of actions taken, that is, reduced cooperation or support for a company (cooperation with partners, access to convenient financial resources, negative attitude of public institutions, and so forth.). This may contribute to constraints in accessing funds necessary for growth from overt sources and provoke resorting to covert sources of capital.

Although the influence of the shadow economy (primarily in the form of undeclared turnover and employment) on the operation and management of SMEs is generally high and varies from company to company in different areas. It influences almost all spheres of company operation (slightly less on organizational changes). Opinions on the scale and direction of that influence vary when it comes to operations and management depending on the actual activity in the shadow economy. Unregistered turnover has a larger influence on the external areas of company operations, which are usually related to attracting external funding, whereas unregistered employment influences internal areas to a larger extent, in particular attracting new personnel and developing existing personnel.

The negative impact of the shadow economy activity is disproportionately high when compared with its positive influence. This can be seen when contracting credit and loans, creating an image, relations with authorities, attracting and developing personnel, and relations with suppliers and customers. The positive influence of the shadow economy on the operation of companies is limited to several areas only, including profitability of activity and cooperation with customers and suppliers. It is more evident in the case of unregistered turnover than unregistered employment.

Operating in the shadow economy negatively influences the capacity of a company to grow in a longer-term perspective, as expressed by 80 percent of entrepreneurs surveyed representing SMEs. The majority of the surveyed in that group believes that in the long run such an operation is more detrimental than favorable in terms of the company's capacity to grow (Figure 2.3). Still, many companies (36.2 percent) recognize positive effects of the shadow economy in terms of their growth, and 10 percent believe that while operating in the shadow economy it is possible to create favorable conditions for developing

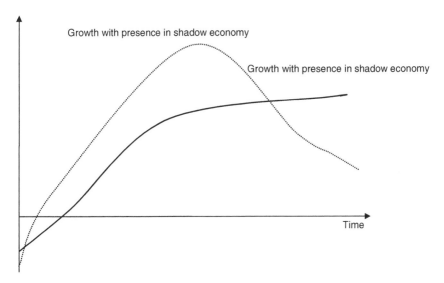

Figure 2.3 Influence of shadow economy on company's growth.
Source: Stos, 2008.

the growth capacity of a firm. The attitude of entrepreneurs regarding the influence of the shadow economy on growth vary depending on the following: motivation and goals, location, scale and market. Entrepreneurs who rationalize their operation in the shadow economy with shortage of capital more frequently refer to advantages of the shadow economy in terms of business growth capacity than do those who point to the shortage of knowledge or experience. Quick success as the main reason for operating in the shadow economy does not have a major influence in business growth capacity. It seems that quick success is insufficient to build growth capacity in a company.

Negative opinions expressed by entrepreneurs about the detrimental effects of operating in the shadow economy apply to all areas of operation and management, regardless the form of shadow economy activity. Positive influence of the shadow economy on the growth capacity is limited to two areas of operation:

- *Assessment of profitability*, which means that investment while operating in the shadow economy is linked with expectations to improve the economic standing of a firm and consequently stimulate growth (many economic efficiency indicators are improved, in particular profitability and liquidity – applicable to combines efficiency, both overt and covert), and
- *Cooperation with customers and suppliers* (more visible in case of unregistered turnover than employment).

Risk of Failure in the Process of Small Businesses' Growth in the Shadow Economy

Operation in the shadow economy diminishes the net profits of a company. This means that, on the one hand, it reduces the level of safe internal growth and sustainable growth and, on the other, it exerts pressure on unsustainable growth, funded by faster growth of external capital rather than retained profit. Although financial capacity is growing, it is growth without resorting to external capital and instead using one's own capital contribution. The latter originates, however, from illegal income, but such capacity cannot be used due to the illegal nature of its source. Consequently, the shadow economy stimulates faster growth than the sustainable growth, namely growth funded from a growing external capital. In reaction to the above, growing external capital involvement reduces the scale of effective presence of the shadow economy in the operation of a company. This can be a self-regulatory mechanism controlling the shadow economy and growth of firms, provided investors focus only on real consequences of the shadow economy. However, it is not the case. Investors concentrate too often on 'apparent effects' of the shadow economy, and thus the role of the regulatory mechanism is diminished, whereas the risk to the efficient use of assets developed due to the investment is growing. It seems that the larger the investment and the higher the presence of the shadow economy in the investment process, the higher is the risk for investment and the higher probability of failure.

That risk is further growing in case of mistakes in management, in particular in finance, personnel and contacts with the environment due to the shortage of competences and experience of small businesses. The shadow economy aggravates crisis situations and hampers efficient restructuring. One of investment success factors is eliminating or reducing the shadow economy. In case no such limitation occurs, operation in the shadow economy may contribute to the economic failure of a company.

Thus, apart from a positive influence on growth of assets, we may observe negative impact of the shadow economy and increased risk of economic failure due to the following factors:

1. Overestimating investment efficiency;
2. Uncontrolled growth of cost related to servicing debt;
3. Mistakes in management;
4. Sanctions in case covert sources of investment funding (our own or others).

The graph below presents negative consequences on the growth of companies of operating in the shadow economy (Figure 2.4).

The shadow economy influences the efficiency of management in different functions, particularly in the middle stage of growth. In the initial and maturity phase, this influence is negligible.

As regards the influence of the shadow economy on motivating, it seems it is positive during survival and success phases only since it is a primary source of funding for financial incentives. In further stages, when motivation systems become more complex and based on participation and loyalty, the shadow economy has a very negative impact, since it makes formal processes more difficult. As long as the owner exercises direct control, the shadow economy should not be a problem. Operating in the shadow economy becomes a barrier with the need to provide the owner's own control.

Effective management of a firm in the process of its growth and development needs to be professional. This requires the following: (a) building of a formal structure of the firm, as early as possible, since the shadow economy makes formal processes difficult and contributes to developing informal structures; (b) introducing decentralized management, since decision making is wide spread over a number of business areas, whereas the shadow economy supports centralized management since delegating authority increases the risk

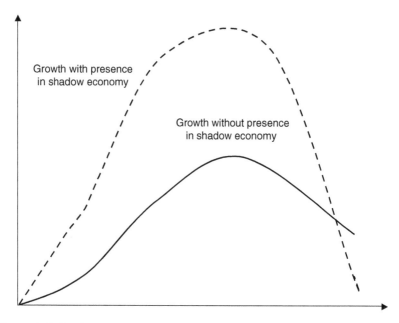

Figure 2.4 Shadow economy, growth of company—failure.
Source: Stos 2009.

of sanctions; (c) development of information systems, since with the development of the company, the information gap is growing, in particular in the area of diagnosing internal crisis situations; however the shadow economy does not support their development, and thus weakens monitoring of crisis symptoms, increasing the risk of late reaction to crises; (d) development of planning processes, since the information absorption capacity depends on the development of planning; however the development of planning necessitates access to all data determining business processes in the future; (e) strengthening indirect owner's control during establishing managerial functions (delegating the running of the business to professional managers). On the one hand, with the growth of the company the role of an indirect owner's supervision is growing as well, exercised from the position of a member of the supervisory board. On the other, the shadow economy strengthens direct supervision typical for an early stage of a company's growth; (f) separation of corporate and property rights, to make the "exit from investment" more efficient through sales of shares rather than liquidation—meanwhile a large part of the shadow economy efficiency influencing the value of company sold is non-disposable, since it is directly linked with the owner leaving the company.

Conclusion

Development-oriented action concentrating on the quick growth of a firm is possible in a company with a large business potential; however, limiting factors are a shortage of its own capital, limited debt capacity and competences of managers. After overcoming the capital barrier, in the implementation of growth strategies when operating in the shadow economy an entrepreneur needs to deal with the high risk related to it and show professionalism in management due to the growing complexity of the growth phase, in particular in the context of obvious poor relations and cooperation with the environment. However, a major change in the attitude and behavior of an entrepreneur can be very difficult. Professionalization (formalization) of management, real delegation of authority and a transparent business control system may extend beyond the capacity of an entrepreneur operating in the shadow economy due to specific features of such an operation (concern about high risk, the covert nature of internal operation, problems with attracting specialists and difficult contact with environment).

The analysis of factors related to implementing investment in assets with a presence in the shadow economy needs to be continued. Findings so far enable the following conclusions:

1. Investment implemented with presence in the shadow economy may result in stagnation and futile growth (growth of assets not followed by increase in income).
2. Efficient growth due to investment in assets (when growth of asserts is accompanied by growth of income at a level that does not reduce their productivity) requires limiting the shadow economy, otherwise the cost of shadow economy operation is growing, for example, "loyalty" costs (internal and external), as well as the growing cost of capital for financing the investment.
3. Risk of economic failure of a firm investing with presence in the shadow economy is growing due to underestimating the efficiency of investment in consequence of including apparent effects in the calculation. The risk is growing also in the case of mistakes in management, in particular management of finance, personnel and contacts with the environment as a result of a shortage of competences and experience in SMEs.

The probability of failure is growing with the size of investment and growth of presence of the shadow economy in financing the investment.

References

Adizes, Ichak (2004). *Managing Corporate Lifecycles.* Santa Barbara: The Adizes Institute Publishing.

Amit, Raphael and Schoemaker, Paul J. (1993). "Strategic assets and organizational rent." *Strategic Management Journal* 14: 33–46.

Argenti, John (1976). *Corporate Collapse.* Berkshire: McGraw-Hill.

Baldwin, John R., Gray, Tara, Johnson, Joanne, Proctor, Jody, Rafiquzzaman, Mohammed and Sabourin, David (1997). *Failing Concerns: Business Bankruptcy in Canada.* Ottawa: Statistics Canada, Minister of Industry.

Baldwin, Robert E. (1995). "The effect of trade and foreign direct investment and relative wages." *OECD Economic Studies* 23: 7–54.

Barney, Jay B. (1991). "Firm resources and sustained competitive advantage." *Journal of Management* 17: 99–120.

———. (2001). "Resource-based theories of competitive advantage: A ten-year retrospective on the resource-based view." *Journal of Management* 6: 643–50.

Bartlett, Will and Buković, Vladimir (2001). "Barriers of SME growth in Slovenia." *Economic Policy in Transition Economies* 11(2): 177–95.

Baum, Robert, Locke, Edwin A. and Smith, Ken G. (2001). "Multidimensional model of venture growth." *The Academy of Management Journal* 44(2): 292–303.

Bleicher, Knut (1991). *Das Konzept integriertes Management.* Frankfurt and New York: St. Galler Managementkonzept, Bd. I.

Blackburn, Robert A., Hart, Mark and Wainwright, Thomas (2013). "Small business performance: business, strategy and owner-manager characteristics." *Journal of Small Business and Enterprise Development* 20(1): 8–27. DOI 10.1108/14626001311298394

Bradley III, Don B. (2000). *Lack of Financial and Location Planning Causes Small Business Bankruptcy,* University of Central Arkansas. http://www.sbaer.uca.edu/research/asbe/2000/10.pdf.

Bullock, Anna, Cosh, Andy, Fu, Xiaolan, Hughes, Alan and Yang, Qing Gong. (2004). *SME Growth Trajectories: A Pilot Study of UK SME Growth and Survival Using the CBR Panel Data.* http://www.berr.gov.uk/files/file38282.pdf.

Business Demography Statistics. http://ec.europa.eu/eurostat/statistics-explained/index.php/Business_demography_statistics#Enterprise_survival_rate.

Caca, Enkela (2010). "The factors influencing SMEs in countries in transition: The Albania case." *International Journal of Interdisciplinary Social Sciences* 5(3): 139–48.

Chandler, Alfred D. (1962), *Strategy and Structure: Chapter in the History of the Industrial Enterprise.* Cambridge, MA: MIT Press.

Chandra, Yanto, Styles, Chris and Wilkinson, Ian (2009). "The recognition of first time international entrepreneurial opportunities: Evidence from firms in knowledge-based industries." *International Marketing Review* 26(1): 30–61.

Central Statistical Office (2007). *Rachunki narodowe według sektorów i podsektorów instytucjonalnych 2000–2005.* Warszawa: Central Statistical Office.

Churchill, Neil C. and Lewis, Virginia L. (1983). "The five stages of small business growth." *Harvard Business Review,* May-June.

Davidsson, Per (1991). "Continued entrepreneurship: Ability, need, and opportunity as determinants of small firm growth." *Journal of Business Venturing* 6(6): 405–29.

Davidsson, Per, Achtenhagen, Leona and Naldi Lucia (2010). "Research on small firm growth: A review." *European Institute of Small Business.*

Djankow, Simeon et al. (2002). "Going informal: Benefits and costs." *World Bank, Working Paper* no 10509: 1–16.

Flamholtz, Eric, and Randle, Yvonne (2007). "Successful organizational development and growing pains." *Management Online Review* March. https://www.mgtsystems.com/sites/default/files/Successful%20Organizational%20Development%20and%20Growing%20Pains.pdf.

Garnsey, Elisabeth, Stam, Erik and Heffernan, Paul (2006). "New Firm Growth: Exploring Processes and Paths." *Industry and Innovation* 13(1): 1–20.

Grant, Robert (1991). "The resource-based theory of competitive advantage: Implications for strategy formulation." *California Management Review* (Spring): 114–35.

Greiner, Larry (1972). "Evolution and revolution as organizations grow." *Harvard Business Review* July–August.

Gupta Priya, Dhamija, Guha, Samapti and Krishnaswami Shiva, Subramanian (2013). "Firm growth and its determinants." *Journal of Innovation and Entrepreneurship: A Systems View Across Time and Space* 2:5. https://doi.org/10.1186/2192-5372-2-15

Henschel, Thomas (2008). *Risk Management Practice for SMEs: Evaluation and Implementation Effective Risk Management System.* Berlin: Erich Schmidt.

Hudson, John et al. (2012). "Evaluating the impact of the informal economy on businesses in South East Europe: Some lessons from the 2009 World Bank Enterprise Survey." *South East European Journal of Economics and Business* 7(1): 99–110. DOI: 10.2478/v10033-012-0010-x

Katz, Jerome A. and Green, Richard, P. (2007). *Entrepreneurial Small Business.* Boston: McGraw-Hill Irwin.

Kelley, Donna and Marriam, Ed (2004). "Managing a growing business." In *The Portable MBA in Entrepreneurship.* Bygrave, William D. and Zacharakis, Andrew (Eds.). Hoboken, NJ: Wiley and Sons, 3rd edn, 405–26.

Levie, Jonathan and Lichtenstein, Benyamin (2010). "A terminal assessment of stages theory: Introducing a dynamic states approach to entrepreneurship." *Entrepreneurship: Theory and Practice* 34(2): 317–50.

Majumdar, Satyajit (2008). "Modelling growth strategy in small entrepreneurial business organisations." *Journal of Entrepreneurship* (September) 17(2): 157–68.

Nelson, Richard and Winter, Sidney (1982). *An Evolutionary Theory of Economic Change.* Cambridge, MA: Belknap Press/Harvard University Press.

O'Farrell, Patrick and Hitchins, David (2002). "*Alternative theories of small firm growth.*" In Morris F. Krueger (Ed.). *Entrepreneurship: Critical Perspectives on Business and Management.* London and New York: Routledge.

Quinn, Robert and Cameron, Kim (1983). "Organizational life cycles and shifting criteria of effectiveness: Some preliminary evidence." *Management Science* 29(1): 33–41.

Ropęga Jaroslaw (2013). "The process of business failure in Polish small enterprises." In *Development of Small and Medium-Sized Enterprises—An International Perspective.* Lodz: SAN.

Ropęga Jaroslaw and Stawasz Edward (2014). "Barriers and Risk Factors in the Development of Micro and Small Businesses in Poland." In *International Entrepreneurship and Corporate Growth in Visegrad Countries* (99–114). A. S. Gubik and K. Wach (Eds.). Miscolc: University of Miscolc.

Schneider, Friedrich (2015). "Size and development of the shadow economy of 31 European and 5 other OECD countries from 2003 to 2015: Different developments." *Journal of Self-Governance and Management Economics* 3(4): 7–29.

Schneider, Friedrich and Enste, Dominik H. (2000). "Shadow sconomies: Size, causes and consequences." *Journal of Economic Literature* 38: 77–114.

Schneider, Friedrich, Raczkowski, Konrad and Mróz, Bogdan (2015). "Shadow economy and tax evasion in the EU." *Journal of Money Laundering Control* 18(1): 34–51.

Shane, Scott (2000). "Prior knowledge and the discovery of entrepreneurial opportunities." *Organization Science* 11(4): 448–69.

Slatter, Stuart and Lovett, David (1999). *Corporate Turnaround.* London: Penguin.

Smallbone, David, Leigh, Robert and North, David (1995). "The characteristics and strategies of fast growth SMEs." *International Journal of Entrepreneurial Behaviour and Research* 1(3): 44–62.

Stos, Daniel (2008). "Wpływ szarej strefy na funkcjonowanie i wzrost przedsiębiorstwa – analiza przypadków." In: *Zarządzanie wzrostem małych i średnich firm zarządzanie wzrostem małych i średnich firm w kontekście szarej strefy.* Stawasz Edward (Ed.). Lodz: University Press.

Stawasz, Edward and Głodek, Paweł (2010). "SMEs innovation and job creation potential in the shadow economy context." *Comparative Economic Research Central and Eastern Europe* 13(4): 99–116.

Storey, David (1994). *Understanding the Small Business Sector.* London: Routledge.

Wiklund, Johan, Patzelt, Holger and Shepherd, Dean (2009). "Building an integrative model of small business growth." *Small Business Economics* 32: 351–74. doi 10.1007/s11187-007-9084-8

Wiklund, Johan (1998). "Small Firm Growth and Performance: Entrepreneurship and Beyond." Doctoral dissertation. Jönköping: Jönköping International Business School.

Williams, Colin (2007). "Small business and the informal economy: Evidence from the UK." *International Journal of Entrepreneurship Behaviour and Research* 13(6): 349–66.

Chapter 3

FAILURE AS A BARRIER TO ENTREPRENEURIAL NEW VENTURING IN NORTHERN IRELAND

Caroline O'Kane

Introduction

Entrepreneurship is acknowledged as an established mechanism for reallocating resources in such a way that promising new, innovative activities replace obsolete activities. Failure is therefore recognized as part of a dynamic, healthy economy in the same way as are other stages in the business lifecycle, such as business creation. There is evidence that the most successful economies across the world play host to more failures—that economies with more churn have faster productivity and economic growth (Fogel et al. 2008). This supports Joseph Schumpeter's (1942) theory of "creative destruction," where stagnant firms wither and die and are replaced by the innovators, who thrive and bloom. Failure is therefore an unavoidable part of economic growth.

Despite this, in many European countries failure tends to be stigmatized, with the failed entrepreneur perceived—rightly or wrongly—as the primary cause of the failure and the demise of the business. Risk is seen as something that should be avoided rather than being an intrinsic element of enterprise. It is rarely the case that failed entrepreneurs are seen to have gained valuable information from their failure and that they may, at some stage, decide to reenter self-employment (Mueller and Niese 2007). This is certainly the case in Northern Ireland, a region GEM (Global Entrepreneurship Monitor) researchers have cited as historically having higher proportions of would-be entrepreneurs reporting fear of failure as a deterrent to starting a business than other UK regions, although rates have been showing improvement in more recent times (Hart et al. 2015). Despite improvements in Northern Ireland with regard to attitudes around fear of failure, differences most definitely remain between Northern Ireland, in particular, the United Kingdom in general and countries such as the United States, where failure is seen as a badge of honor or a rite of passage in order to learn lessons and achieve future success.

In the UK's current economic climate, entrepreneurs are needed more than ever to innovate, create jobs and generate wealth, and a clear economic and social rationale exists for helping entrepreneurs with previous failure experiences to seek out positive experiences from their negative failure, as businesses set up by restarters grow faster than first-timers in terms of turnover and jobs created (Stam et al. 2006). However, in order to exploit the full potential of all would-be entrepreneurs, society must become more accepting of failure and offer "honest failures" the support and opportunity for a fresh start, which will contribute both to a personal renaissance and to the rebuilding and rebalancing of the wider economy.

This chapter explores fear of failure—which historically has been particularly high in Northern Ireland—as a deterrent to entrepreneurial new venturing, and considers ways in which fear of failure may become less of a hindering factor for future would-be entrepreneurs than it has been previously.

Defining Business Failure

Despite representing a significant outcome of entrepreneurial activity, literature on entrepreneurial failure is limited. In particular, entrepreneurship after a previous failure is an especially underdeveloped area of research.

In addition, the concept of failure is difficult to define, mainly because academics, government policy makers, the media and society all tend to define business failure in different ways. According to John Watson and Jim Everett (1993), it is important to be clear about the definitions used when exploring the subject of failure. M. Scott and Jane Lewis (1984) concur, stating "the root cause of our difficulties […] is the careless use of the word 'failure' and its several synonyms—death, discontinuance, insolvency, bankruptcy" (30).

Business failure has been defined in a number of different ways. For instance, a broad definition of failure views it as "firms which were liquidated or sold to avoid loss" (Ulmer and Nelson 1947: 11). Watson and Everett (1993), reporting on the work of Cochran (1981), also touch on the subject of loss, defining failure as "an inability to make a go of it, whether losses entail one's own capital, or someone else's, or indeed, any capital." According to Dean Shepherd et al. (2000), business failure reflects "the probability that a firm will become insolvent and be unable to recover from that insolvency before being bankrupt and ceasing operations" (396).

Another term that needs clarity is "discontinuance," a concept that may not also be synonymous with failure. For instance, business discontinuance can come about both for positive reasons—the business may be sold at a profit—as well as for negative reasons—including retirement or illness (Cochran 1981).

In addition, there is confusion in terms of defining what is meant by "failure" in general and in wider society, as evidence and attitudes from the United States make their way to European shores. For instance, there are those who state that a failure experience nurtures self-management abilities, the skill to cope with setbacks and the ability to boost human strength in terms of vitality, resilience and restoration (Byrne et al. 2011), generating a "rich personal and professional learning experience" (3).

In this chapter, business failure is viewed as the ceasing of a business brought about by predicted or actual losses, or another outcome that did not meet initial expectations, as opposed to the wider concept of discontinuance, which might not necessarily have the same level of emotional, behavioral or economic impact on the failed entrepreneur.

Main Issues Affecting Individuals with Previous Failure Experience

Academic researchers and practitioners working with second-chance entrepreneurs have identified the main areas where the key barriers and impediments facing business restarts frequently appear after an earlier failure: the cultural aspect, the financial aspect and the educational aspect.

Cultural aspect: Tackling fear of failure

Fear of failure is believed to be particularly apparent at start-up, being a critical factor in aspirant entrepreneurs deciding whether or not to pursue entrepreneurial activities in the first place (Minniti et al. 2005). This fear arises from a number of different sources, including the assessment of financial, psychological and social risks (Hisrich and Brush 1986).

Literature suggests that serial entrepreneurs are less likely to fear failure, even if they have previous failure experience, since they repeatedly turn to self-employment despite knowing the risk and uncertainty attached to the start-up process (Mueller and Niese 2007). Reporting on the work of Wagner (2003), the authors suggest that individuals who are less afraid of failure are more likely to make an entrepreneurial restart.

Although statistics on fear of failure for second-chance entrepreneurs in Northern Ireland are not available, GEM research has shown that the region has consistently had the highest fear of failure rate in the UK—for instance, in 2013, 49.5 percent of the non-entrepreneurial adult population reported that fear of failure would prevent them from starting a business (Hart et al. 2014).

Cultural aspect: Challenging negative attitudes toward failed entrepreneurs

Recovery from failure is something of a healing process, requiring the failed entrepreneur to overcome not only the financial loss of the business, but also feelings of shame: either because of how they believe they are perceived by others, or because of social stigma they may actually experience from others. Others grieve for the business they have lost, with many experiencing emotions similar to bereavement or a close relationship ending (Watson and Newby 2005). Recovery from business failure occurs when the entrepreneur reemerges after this time of "mourning" and self-reflection and begins to repair the damage of personal and professional relationships with the support of those around them (Cope 2011). The ability of the failed entrepreneur to overcome emotional, psychological and practical barriers and take steps toward a second chance at business ownership is more likely to develop if they receive social affirmation (Byrne et al. 2011; Cope 2011).

However, it is acknowledged that entrepreneurship "requires an environment that is conducive to business. [...] This enabling environment [...] depends on society recognizing the role that business plays and welcoming, rather than shunning, entrepreneurs" (Irwin 2005: 5). In order for enterprise to thrive and grow, the culture of a community, region or country needs to support individuals who possess the confidence, abilities and drive to pursue entrepreneurial careers, whether for the first time or after previous failures. Although determining an exact definition is problematic due to its shifting nature, Alison Morrison (2000) describes culture as "a shared, collective way groups of people understand and interpret the world" (60) while, according to Malach-Pines et al. (2005), "culture is learned and is manifested through heroes, symbols, rituals and values" (543). Cultural values and beliefs, including perceptions of entrepreneurship and entrepreneurs and prevailing attitudes toward success and failure, are believed to shape the behavior of citizens and influence decisions to engage in entrepreneurial activity (Verheul et al. 2004).

It is acknowledged that regions with strong traditions of entrepreneurial new venturing, where entrepreneurship is respected and failure is not stigmatized, have an advantage over those where it is viewed with hostility or suspicion in terms of perpetuating its development and growth across generations (Mueller 2006). According to Robertson et al. (2003), negative social and cultural attitudes toward entrepreneurship—including views on new venture creation, wealth generation and fear of failure—present significant barriers to business start-up and growth on a wider scale.

This puts Northern Ireland at a disadvantage. The region has been shown to historically have had an "entrepreneurial deficit" compared with most other areas of the UK (Hart 2006). Findings suggest that NI's culture is itself an impediment to environment, with evidence of a less well-developed culture for entrepreneurship (Fitzsimons and O'Gorman 2003) and a strong cultural resistance to entrepreneurial activity; for example, risk-taking is not encouraged and role models are not immediately apparent.

A lack of positive cultural support for entrepreneurship has been cited as the one of the main obstacles preventing a greater level of entrepreneurial activity in Northern Ireland. Partial explanation for this might lie with findings that suggest that negative attitudes toward entrepreneurship are more likely to be held in areas of high social deprivation (Slack 2005) or those with a high reliance on social security benefits (Martz et al. 2003), as is the case in benefits-dependent Northern Ireland. In addition, a region's culture is also believed to be affected if the area has a strong history of public-sector employment (Chigunta 2002). In Northern Ireland there has been a long-standing overreliance on the public sector as a driver of economic growth, accounting for 27.9 percent of total employment in 2013 compared to 17.4 percent in England (ONS 2014), and which may have a dampening effect on potential entrepreneurs by providing safe, secure employment and making them risk-averse (Fitzsimons et al. 2005). The dominance of the public sector in Northern Ireland can be traced back to "a wholly unique set of conditions [...] terrorism, civil unrest, political instability" (First Trust Bank 2006: 18).

According to numerous studies, European entrepreneurs frequently have to contend with a number of preconceived notions and opinions, including implications that those successful in business have low morals or ethics (Small Business Service 2004); that society generally resents those who are successful (Irwin 2001) or views them with a degree of suspicion (Guthrie 2006). Compared to the United States, where entrepreneurs are celebrated and held up as role models, even if they have failed, entrepreneurs in the UK are "resented for being successful or stigmatized when they fail. Perhaps that is why people in the UK are more risk-averse than [people] in many other countries" (Irwin 2005: 8).

These attitudes seem to prevail whether business failure is due to external circumstances that are beyond the control of the entrepreneur (decreasing demand for products/services, economic crisis, entrance of a new competitor) or due to personal incompetence. Further, for those entrepreneurs who have failed, the attitudes they encounter in others may be compounded by any number of negative emotional responses they personally experience—grief, shame, anger, guilt and so on.

Social and cultural conditioning, therefore, appears to confuse professional and personal failure in the minds both of the failed entrepreneur and those they encounter, frequently leading them to withdraw from the idea of an entrepreneurial career and to seek out what are perceived to be safer, paid employment options.

Tackling finance as a barrier to restart

Business failure impacts entrepreneurs across every dimension of their personal and professional lives, with one of the most being a negative impact on finances. According to Singh et al. (2007), the failed entrepreneur has to deal with the impact of the sudden loss of income combined with the pressure to repay financial obligations; further, if the debt is significant or is owed to public institutions or banks, it may be made public and be compounded by personal feelings of shame and embarrassment.

Access to finance and difficulties arising from liquidity constraints are considered major factors influencing whether entrepreneurs will go on to start their own businesses (Tonoyan et al. 2005), whether for the first time or following a previous failure. There are two schools of thought regarding access to finance for the entrepreneur who is starting again after a previous failure. On one hand, there are suggestions that an entrepreneurial restarter has better access to financial capital, as previous entrepreneurial performance helps generate this through their enhanced social networks (Hayward et al. 2010). However, if the entrepreneur owes money from their previous failure, a poor credit rating makes it unlikely they will be able to restart, particularly if their failure involved losses with a bank or other external creditor (Byrne et al. 2011).

For those seeking a second chance at entrepreneurship in Northern Ireland, the situation may be even more problematic. Aspirant entrepreneurs in the region have been shown to be more likely to be dissuaded from pursuing their ambitions because of lack of funding than are those in any other UK region. Compounded by bankruptcy laws that treat "honest failures" as if they were fraudulent, this creates—for those with previous failure experience—even more difficulty accessing finance to support a restart.

The need to change perceptions through education

Education provides the basis for shaping the knowledge, behavior and orientation of individuals: "Education is a critical shaper of attitudes. How one is educated today will determine the success of tomorrow" (Birdthistle 2008: 554).

Enterprise education provides benefits to wider society beyond its function supporting new business ventures (European Commission 2004; Kolvereid and Moen 1997). For instance, enterprise education not only helps aspirant entrepreneurs accumulate skills and knowledge useful for new venture creation, but it also teaches skills vital for life, not just business ownership (Davidsson and Honig 2003); this education also plays an important role in fostering under-standing and respect for entrepreneurship, helping overcome cultural barriers to the development of enterprise (Murray and White 1986).

However, despite knowing that lessons from one failed business can be car-ried forward to influence another new venture, the ability of a failed entrepre-neur to use these lessons and to develop competencies that help with a restart, depend very much on a number of circumstances. For instance, entrepreneurs with failure experience are unlikely to be in the frame of mind to learn lessons from that failure if they are weighed down by feelings frequently associated with loss, such as grief, pain and remorse at what has gone wrong and what they should have done differently (Byrne et al. 2011; Cope 2011). It is import-ant that they are given the time, distance and support to emerge from this self-imposed period of reflection if they are to come back stronger and seek a renaissance of their entrepreneurial dream.

Methodology

Since 2014, the author has been working on the Value of Failure project, a transnational Erasmus+ research study that seeks to develop opportunities and give those with previous failure experience a second chance at entrepreneurial success in three European regions: Poland, Germany and Northern Ireland.[1] The project seeks to improve the environment for second-chance entrepre-neurs by challenging preconceived attitudes to failure, addressing access to finance as a barrier to second-chance entrepreneurship and developing tools for failure to be incorporated into Higher Education Training and Vocational Education and Training (VET) offerings.

The Second Chance Entrepreneurs Alliance Toolkit (Markiewicz and Gracz 2015), comprising a program of learning actions and guidance on how to support second-chance entrepreneurship, was developed at the program's outset as a means of assisting other regions to roll the project out in their own areas. The toolkit also guided partners in establishing Second Chance Entrepreneurs Alliances in Poland, Germany and Northern Ireland. The Alliances are comprised of stakeholders, including local authorities, VET providers/trainers, policy makers, enterprise support organizations, further and higher education institutions and banks—and of entrepreneurs with previous failure experience who have restarted and are willing to share their

---

1   Project partners: University of Szczecin, Poland (project leaders); TheVisionWorks (Germany); Enterprise Northern Ireland (NI); Canice Consulting Ltd (NI); CreoMind (Poland)

experiences with others. In each region, Alliance members have attended a series of plenary meetings, each meeting examining a different theme relating to second-chance entrepreneurship, including an exploration of perceptions and knowledge of the current situation affecting second-chance entrepreneurs in each region, including the policy environment and public opinion; sharing best practices and solutions that help encourage second-chance entrepreneurship. The plenary meeting process ended with the signing of an action plan, detailing the collaborative action required to increase the levels of second-chance entrepreneurship in each region.

In acknowledgment of the fact that "self-efficacy can be developed through vicarious experience [...] through exposure to the experiences of others" (Cooper and Lucas 2006: 145), entrepreneurs who had faced earlier failures but had managed to start new businesses were encouraged to attend and tell their stories, inspiring those who perhaps were undecided about pursuing a second chance while reassuring finance/enterprise support providers that efforts to assist those seeking a second chance are worthwhile.

Further, in order to support the development of action plans and high-quality teaching and training materials, interviews have also been held in each region with "real life" failed entrepreneurs—those who have emerged from a failure experience, set up new business and are willing to go public with their stories.

In Northern Ireland, interviews were guided by the qualitative research methodology. One of the strengths of this methodology lies in its ability to "get under the surface in order to understand people's perceptions and experiences" (Silverman 2006: 5). Mason (2002) concurs: "Through qualitative research we can explore a wide array of dimensions of the social world, including [...] the understandings, experiences and imaginings of our research participants, the ways that social processes, institutions, discourses or relationships work, and the significance of the meanings that they generate" (1).

Krauss (2005) describes qualitative research as a highly intuitive activity, seeking to construct meaning and achieve new knowledge and information. As the interviews were conducted to explore, clarify and discover new insights into the individual experiences of failed entrepreneurs in terms of identifying barriers encountered when they attempted an entrepreneurial restart—and to take into consideration their private thoughts and feelings—a qualitative approach was considered the most appropriate way forward.

In order to get close to interviewees to explore their experiences, feelings and attitudes with sensitivity and compassion, and to gain insight into fear of failure as a barrier to interviewees while pursuing an entrepreneurial renaissance, semi-structured in-depth interviews were used to collect narrative data. The value of this approach was that it offered an "appropriate means for gathering complex and sensitive information" (Hair et al. 2003: 142) as required by this project.

Specifically, the semi-structured interview process adopted, in which a range of topics and questions provide a basis for the interview, allows participants to articulate both their thoughts and feelings on a range of issues as well as to build upon initial responses in order to develop unexpected issues. The technique enables researchers to probe for further information, to vary the order of questions or ask new questions, depending upon replies given (Saunders et al. 2007; Mason 2002), or to ask supplementary questions in order to confirm or expand upon issues raised by interviewees. These techniques were used when the researcher needed to adapt the line of questioning to earlier responses, meaning each plenary meeting and interview session remained flexible to embrace newly emergent themes or issues.

In order for business failure to be seen as a stepping stone to second-chance entrepreneurship, a major element of the Value of Failure project was the development of teaching materials for higher-education lecturers to deliver to third-level students, and training materials for VET trainers to deliver to second-chance entrepreneurs. Some of the learning resources, including modules on risk assessment and minimization strategies, are also applicable to first-time entrepreneurs. Given findings within extant literature that the current education system emphasizes exam success, focusing on the learning of general concepts, theories and paradigms rather than promoting a more enterprising approach to learning (Martinez et al. 2007), the Value of Failure course is innovative in that it invites participants to consider the prospect of failure in its broadest sense and in many different aspects of life, not just in the business context. By requiring course participants to actively think about failure, the educational tools aim to demystify failure and to remove the stigma and negative attitudes toward it.

The development of these tools is crucially important. First-time entrepreneurs can rely on significant amounts of support for business start-up, but there is an acknowledged lack of support for second-chance entrepreneurs who have different support and information needs than first-time entrepreneurs. However, most VET providers continue to offer a uniform service, the content of which has remained largely unchanged for a decade or more. The Value of Failure project seeks to revolutionize current VET provision to ensure that the businesses established by second-chance entrepreneurs are guided properly to facilitate learning effectively from the past.

The Value of Failure project can kickstart the development of a comprehensive and integrated approach to second-chance entrepreneurship by constructing tailor-made training and support for them, mainstreaming that training across relevant stakeholders at the regional level. The course content is itself innovative and based upon innovative pedagogic strategies and learning approaches, such as the flipped classroom model, improved learner integration and the story-based learning approach.

Enterprise education is known to play an important role in reinforcing positive attitudes toward entrepreneurship (Eureka Strategic Research 2003). The educational tools created by the Value of Failure project encourage participants to think about failure in all walks of life, and to view it as potentially bringing value and benefits to their future learning, growth and development. This should help aspirant entrepreneurs realize that if their business ideas do not work out, it is not the end of the world, while alerting those comprising their social and professional networks that business closure does not equate with personal failure nor with all the punishment and retribution it currently often brings to many.

The research team recommends that trainers and educators expand their range of pedagogies to reflect new and innovative approaches to teaching and learning, including the use of role models, guest speakers, teaching materials and case studies based on real businesses. For instance, "the use of guest entrepreneurs in the classroom provides students with the opportunity to learn from those with first-hand experience of the new venture creation process[; …] exposure to such entrepreneurial role models provides students with the opportunity to gain a sense of the feasibility and desirability of pursuing a similar course of action, learn of likely challenges along the way, as well as hear about ways and means of overcoming them" (Cooper and Lucas 2006: 146). The Value of Failure team particularly recommends the use of role models whose businesses have failed, because "students need exposure to those entrepreneurs who have paid the price, faced the challenges, and endured the failures" (Kuratko 2005: 589).

As part of the dissemination of the Value of Failure project, an online platform has been made available through which teaching, learning and training materials can be downloaded; the aim is to help encourage other regions across Europe to establish Second Chance Entrepreneurs Alliances of their own and thereby contribute to the creation of a better environment for second-chance entrepreneurs across the European Union.

Key interview findings

Although many second-chance entrepreneurs attended the series of plenary meetings, and were willing to sign up as stakeholders of the Second Chance Entrepreneurs Alliance for Northern Ireland, the local research team encountered difficulties in getting entrepreneurs with a previous failure experience to participate in interviews. The majority invited to participate were reluctant to be interviewed, giving reasons for their reticence including "I'm too busy"; "I'm embarrassed by what happened"; and "I don't want to be defined by my failure."

Comments illustrating the key findings are taken from plenary meetings with stakeholders, face-to-face interviews or telephone interviews conducted with entrepreneurs who started or are contemplating a restart after an earlier failure.

Cultural attitudes

Social stigma attached to failure was a key reason why the majority of those invited refused to be interviewed. During the plenary sessions, some described that having established new businesses, they were perceived as being upstanding members of their local business community, holding positions of responsibility within business networks and so on, yet none of their existing business contacts knew about their earlier failure. One female entrepreneur described her reluctance to be interviewed because she had deliberately not told anyone in her network about her earlier failure as she didn't "want them to judge me, to think badly of me."

Another female entrepreneur said it had taken her a long time to come to terms with her business failure, and that people were only just starting to treat her like a "normal" person again; she therefore feared going public with her failure would be a backwards step in terms of her confidence and how she viewed herself. She agreed to be interviewed on condition that her identity was kept confidential. During the interview, she described how, when her first business failed, that friends and family treated her differently from how they had before—some spoke to her in hushed tones, afraid to mention what had happened in case she got upset, whilst others went out of their way to avoid her if they saw her in the street. She presumed they acted like this out either out of embarrassment and a reluctance to talk to her in case she broke down if they mentioned her "failed" business, or because they were afraid her "failure" would somehow taint them.

Another described how he had ceased trading with his first business after 18 months when he realized it was not going to be as profitable as he had hoped—he admitted he had been over-ambitious and over-confident in his ability to run his own business. After a period of paid employment, he was made redundant and had decided to try again with a different business idea. He described how his parents told him they would have preferred him to keep claiming welfare benefits rather than "risking everything and bringing shame on yourself again" if this business similarly failed. He believed their concern was because his first business closing had impacted both on his finances and his self-belief, but felt it was misplaced and misjudged.

Comparisons with cultural attitudes toward failure in the United States were frequently raised. One entrepreneur said, "if you fail in the UK, people just see you as a failure, they can't get past that. If you fail in the US, people see you as someone who has tried." The belief was that, in Northern Ireland, negative attitudes toward entrepreneurs in general, and those who have failed in particular, mean that less people are encouraged to consider an entrepreneurial career, either for the first time or particularly after a previous failure.

However, despite GEM researchers stating that that entrepreneurship flourishes when entrepreneurs are respected rather than viewed with suspicion, there was a consensus that this was unlikely to happen "anytime soon" in Northern Ireland. Attendees at one plenary session believed there was too much going against entrepreneurs in the region that they couldn't see an imminent change in attitudes. For instance, participants believed there was little promotion of local entrepreneurs on TV business stories (apart from when they were facing closure), little in the way of enterprise education for all students, and too much of a focus by government and economic development organizations on big business and attracting Foreign Direct Investment.

Access to finance

Access to finance was perhaps unsurprisingly a key topic for participants and interviewees. Second-chance entrepreneurs, without exception, found it difficult to access finance to support their new business start-up costs, even when the failure or closure of their earlier business had nothing to do with personal incompetence or fraud.

For one entrepreneur, the failure of his business came about as a result of his domestic mortgage being in negative equity—he decided to sell his business and relocate to Northern Ireland from England due to lower costs of living. However, when he attempted to start a similar business in Northern Ireland, he had to finance start-up costs by family members securing loans on his behalf. Others reported being turned down for business loans but instead offered extended overdraft facilities, whilst another had turned to invoice selling to assist with cashflow.

The consensus was that banks in Northern Ireland were themselves, just like the general population, too risk averse, and that they needed to be educated on the reasons why second-chance entrepreneurs deserve help and support.

Education

With regard to education, interviewees and plenary meeting attendees felt that the education system generally failed those who were interested in starting their own business, even those who had studied third level business-related qualifications.

For instance, one attendee was in the process of starting a new business having graduated nine months earlier with a Business Studies degree which, she believed, had failed to prepare her for a career in self-employment as it was aimed almost entirely at employment within the private and public sector. She had, during the four years of her degree, completed only one module focused on self-employment which was focused almost exclusively on developing a business plan. Although other modules had been useful in providing a background to accounts and marketing, and soft skills such as coping with a heavy workload, determination, motivation and making presentations, she felt that the degree had largely been a waste of time in terms of preparing her for an entrepreneurial career. A further new entrepreneur had recently graduated with a degree in marketing, and was similarly disappointed that her course only had one taught module related to entrepreneurship. She believed this was not enough to prepare anyone for self-employment although acknowledged that it might have been enough to stir interest in someone who had a vague idea of ultimately owning their own business.

Neither of these new entrepreneurs felt that the modules they had studied during their degree programs adequately reflected—or even touched upon— the subject of entrepreneurial failure. They both believed that the modules they had studied with regard to entrepreneurial new venturing focused on academic definitions, entrepreneurial behaviors and traits and the business planning process rather than reflecting on the reality of entrepreneurial life. Neither felt that failure was dealt with in any great detail, apart from cultural comparisons between the US and Northern Ireland and a brief discussion of options for exit strategies which included knowing when to get out if things were going badly. There was, they said, no discussion around what comes next should a business fail, or how someone could pursue second-chance entrepreneurship.

Participants overwhelmingly believed that entrepreneurship modules should be included on both a compulsory and optional basis on *all* degree courses, and not reserved for those studying business-related qualifications, acknowledging that education contributes toward changing negative attitudes. A number of plenary meeting attendees who had previously studied business-related qualifications (business studies, marketing, accounting) felt that teaching materials should provide a more accurate reflection of the reality of entrepreneurship, including the prospect and implications of failure. They felt that their lectures had, on the whole, been "too staid" and "too formal," and that "enterprise education should be offered in a more enterprising way itself," calling for greater use of local entrepreneurs as guest speakers. In addition, attendees felt that in order for students to get an accurate picture of the reality of business ownership, that guest speakers should not just come from the ranks of those who had succeeded but should include entrepreneurs who had failed and were willing to talk about how things had gone wrong. Further, a recent graduate suggested that students should, if they wish, be able to avail of "entrepreneurial apprenticeships during placement years." Describing her year out as "hell," she related how she had been confined to low-level administrative duties: "receptionist, photocopier, tea-maker," and believed she had missed out on the opportunity to spend her year out with someone "dynamic and truly entrepreneurial who could have taught me about the skills and behaviors needed to develop a business idea and contacts for the future." The introduction of innovative approaches to enterprise education, and the recognition of failure as part of the enterprise curriculum, would undoubtedly play a vital role in the development of an entrepreneurial skills-set that could be utilized by the entrepreneur, either at the time of business start-up, or restart, if applicable.

Conclusion

The reluctance of entrepreneurs to speak publicly about their experiences, even though they have subsequently restarted and made a success of their new business, demonstrates the damaging and long-term effect social stigma can have on an individual who has previous entrepreneurial failure experience. This was demonstrated in one instance by a female entrepreneur who refused to take part in the interviews because the word *failure* was in the project title. In her words: "Yes, my business closed. Yes, it didn't work out. To me, it does not constitute failure, and I am not a failure, I learned lots from that time and it made me come back better and stronger."

However, there is cause for some optimism. Young people in Northern Ireland are more likely than their UK counterparts to participate in activities at school, college or university that made them consider starting a business in the future (Hart et al. 2015). With fear of failure appearing to have become less of a hindering factor in Northern Ireland in recent times than it was previously, it is to be hoped that improvements in the business and cultural environment emanating from the Value of Failure project will combine with high quality, early stage enterprise education and encourage more entrepreneurs in general, and in particular those with a previous failure experience, to start their own business.

In order to tackle fear of failure as a barrier to involvement in new venturing, sustained and sustainable cultural and institutional change is required across the board. For instance, it is to be hoped that, in the future, entrepreneurs with previous failure experiences are not stigmatized because those they come into contact with will no longer confuse professional failure with personal failure. Similarly, it is a goal that education and enterprise support providers will no longer offer a uniform service to all entrepreneurs, but instead will recognize that second-chance entrepreneurs have different support and information needs than first-time entrepreneurs.

The Value of Failure project has been working to optimize the contribution of second-chance entrepreneurs to the economy. This paper demonstrates the importance of fear of failure as an area of study in terms of raising awareness and contributing toward changing enterprise policy priorities. By drawing attention to fear of failure as a barrier to new venturing, and by identifying potential remedies to the entrepreneurial environment emerging from the Value of Failure project, it is hoped that improvements will be made that will assist future generations of entrepreneurs with a previous failure experience to engage in new venture creation second-time around.

References

Birdthistle, Naomi (2008). "An examination of tertiary students' desire to found an enterprise." *Education and Training* 50(7): 552–67.

Byrne, Orla, Mullen, Hellen, Marlow, S. and Mason, C. (2011). "Repeat entrepreneurship following business closure." Working Paper 01-11, University of Strathclyde Business School.

Chigunta, Francis (2002). *Youth Entrepreneurship: Meeting the Key Policy Challenges*. Oxford: Oxford University Press.

Cochran, A. B. (1981). "Small business mortality rates: A review of the literature." *Journal of Small Business Management* 19(4): 50–59.

Cooper, Sarah and Lucas, W. A. (2006). "Developing self-efficacy for innovation and entrepreneurship: An educational approach." *International Journal of Entrepreneurship Education* 4: 141–62.

Cope, Jason (2011). "Entrepreneurial learning from failure." *Journal of Business Venturing* 26(6): 604–23.

Davidsson, Per and Honig, Benson (2003). "The role of social and human capital among nascent entrepreneurs." *Journal of Business Venturing* 18: 301–31.

Eureka Strategic Research (2003). "Youth Entrepreneurship: Scoping Paper." Australia: Department of Family and Community Services.

European Commission (2004). *Final Report of the Expert Group "Education for Entrepreneurship": Making Progress in Promoting Entrepreneurial Attitudes and Skills through Primary and Secondary Education*. Brussels: European Commission.

First Trust Bank (2006). *Economic Outlook and Business Review* 21(1), March. NI: First Trust Bank.

Fitzsimons, Paula and O'Gorman, Colm (2003). *How Entrepreneurial is Ireland? The Global Entrepreneurship Monitor 2003, The Irish Report*. Dublin: Department of Business Administration, University College Dublin.

Fogel, Kathy, Morck, Randall and Yeung, Bernard (2008). "Big business stability and economic growth: Is what's good for General Motors good for America?" *Journal of Financial Economics* 89(1): 83–108.

Guthrie, Jonathan (2006). "Teaching 'vital' to start-ups." *Financial Times*, Entrepreneurship Section (November 13): 4.

Hayward, Mathew L. A., Forster, William R., Sarasvathy, Saras D. and Fredrickson, Barbara L. (2011). "Beyond hubris: How highly confident entrepreneurs rebound to venture again." *Journal of Business Venturing* 25(6): 569–78.

Hart, Mark (2006). *GEM Northern Ireland Summary 2006*. NI: Invest.

Hart, Mark, Bonner, Karen and Levie, Jonathan (2014). *GEM: Northern Ireland Report 2013*. NI: Invest.

———. (2015). *GEM: Northern Ireland Report 2014*. NI: Invest.

Hisrich, Robert D. and Brush, Candida G. (1986). *The Woman Entrepreneur: Starting, Financing, and Managing a Successful New Business*." 2nd edn. Lexington, MA: D. C. Heath & Co.

Irwin, D. (2001). *Stimulating Entrepreneurship*. UK: Small Business Service.

———. (2005). *Breaking Down the Barriers to Business*. UK: Royal Society for the Encouragement of Arts, Manufacturers and Commerce.

Kolvereid, L. and Moen, Ø. (1997). "Entrepreneurship among business graduates: Does a major in entrepreneurship make a difference?" *Journal of European Industrial Training* 21(4): 154–60.

Krauss, S. E. (2005). "Research paradigms and meaning making: A primer." *The Qualitative Report* 10(4): 758–70.

Kuratko, D. F. (2005). "The emergence of entrepreneurship education: Development, trends and challenges." *Entrepreneurship Theory and Practice* (September): 577–97.

Malach-Pines, A., Levy, H. Utasi, A. and Hill, T. L. (2005). "Entrepreneurs as cultural heroes: A cross-cultural, interdisciplinary perspective." *Journal of Managerial Psychology* 20(6): 541–55

Markiewicz, Joanna and Gracz, Leszek (2015). Second Chance Entrepreneurs Alliance (SEAL) Toolkit (draft). Erasmus+ project: Value of Failure, 2014-1-PL01-KA200-003434

Martinez, D., Mora, J. and Vila, L. E. (2007). "Entrepreneurs, the self-employed and employees amongst young European higher education graduates." *European Journal of Education* 42(1): 99–117.

Mason, J. (2002). *Qualitative Researching*, 2nd edn. London: Sage.

Minniti, M., Arenius, P. and Langowitz, N. (2005). *Global Entrepreneurship Monitor 2004 Report on Women and Entrepreneurship*. MA: Center for Women's Leadership.

Morrison, Alison (2000). "Entrepreneurship: What triggers it?" *International Journal of Entrepreneurial Behaviour and Research* 6(2): 59–71.

Mueller, Pamela and Niese, Michael (2007). "Entrepreneurship: Only a Few are Chosen but Some are Even Chosen Twice." In *Empirical Entrepreneurship in Europe: New Perspectives*. Dowling, M. and Schmude, J. (Eds.). Edward Elgar.

Mueller, Pamela (2006). "Entrepreneurship in the region: Breeding ground for nascent entrepreneurs?" *Small Business Economics* 27: 41–58.

Murray, J. A. and White, Anthony (Eds.). (1986). *Education for Enterprise: An Irish Perspective*. Dublin: National Council for Educational Awards and Industrial Development Authority of Ireland.

Office for National Statistics (ONS) (2014). *Compendium of UK Statistics*. UK.

Robertson, Martyn, Collins, Amanda, Medeira, Natasha and Slater, James (2003). "Barriers to start-up and their effect on aspirant entrepreneurs." *Education and Training* 45(6): 308–16.

Saunders, Mark, Lewis, Philip and Thornhill, Adrian (2007). *Research Methods for Business Students*. 4th edn. UK: Prentice Hall.

Scott, M. and Lewis, Jane (1984). "Re-thinking entrepreneurial failure." In *Success and Failure in Small Business*. Jane Lewis, J. Stanworth and A. Gibb (Eds.). Hampshire: Gower.

Shepherd, Dean A., Douglas, Evan J. and Shanley, Mark (2000). "New venture survival: Ignorance, external shocks, and risk reduction strategies." *Journal of Business Venturing* 15: 393–410.

Silverman, David (2006). *Interpreting Qualitative Data: Methods for Analyzing Talk, Text and Interaction*. 3rd edn. UK: Sage.

Singh, Smita, Corner, Patricia Doyle and Pavlovich, Kathryn (2007). "Coping with entrepreneurial failure." *Journal of Management and Organisation* 13(4): 331–44.

Slack, Jonathan (2005). "The New entrepreneur scholarships: Self-employment as a means to tackle social deprivation." *Education and Training* 47(6), 447–55.

Small Business Service (2004). *A Government Action Plan for Small Business: The Evidence Base*. UK: DTI.

Stam, Erik, Audretsch, David and Meijaard, Joris (2008). "Renascent entrepreneurship." *Journal of Evolutionary Economics* 18(3–4): 493–507.

Tonoyan, Vartuhi, Strohmeyer, Robert and Wittman, Werner W. (2005). "Gendered and cross-country differences in the perceived difficulty of becoming self-employed: The impact of individual resources and institutional restrictions." Proceedings of the 25th Annual Entrepreneurship Research Conference.

Ulmer, Melville J. and Neilson, Alice (1947). "Business turnovers and causes of failure." *Survey of Current Business* (April): 10–16.

Value of Failure project website: www.valueoffailure.com

Verheul, Ingrid, van Stel, Andre and Thurik, Roy (2004). *Explaining Male and Female Entrepreneurship Across 29 Countries*. The Netherlands: EIM Business and Policy Research.

Watson, John, and Everett, Jim (1993). "Defining small business failure." *International Small Business Journal* 11(3): 35–48.

Watson, John and Newby, Rick (2005). "Biological sex, stereotypical sex-roles, and SME owner characteristics." *International Journal of Entrepreneurial Behaviour and Research* 11(2): 129–43.

Chapter 4

BUSINESS AND SUSTAINABILITY: KEY DRIVERS FOR BUSINESS SUCCESS AND BUSINESS FAILURE FROM THE PERSPECTIVE OF SUSTAINABLE DEVELOPMENT

Magdalena Ziolo, Filip Fidanoski, Kiril Simeonovski,
Vladimir Filipovski and Katerina Jovanovska

Introduction

Recently, the nature of firms has changed from traditional to sustainable, along with multi-attribute optimizers (profit, people and planet), thus generating financial, social and environmental returns (Emerson, 2003; Soppe, 2004). Sustainable investment funds are allocated to firms according to their attitude towards the environment and their implementation of social sustainability. An increasing number of corporate clients are interested in sustainable financial products. Sustainable building and sustainable energy are two rapidly growing markets. The new energy infrastructure requires the investment of large sums of money. Following multilateral funds for sustainability, such as Global Environment Facility (GEF), Renewable Energy and Energy Efficiency Fund (REEF), SDG (Solar Development Group) and Prototype Carbon Fund (PCF) were established to address global environmental issues in developing countries (Jeucken, 2001).

The decline of the housing, equity, and debt markets prompted the need for accrued regulation, transparency and proper governance. Therefore, the debt sector, as well as the sector of socially responsible investment,[1] and

---

1 SRI has grown dramatically over the past decade. SRI is a booming market globally. As of 2008 it had a worth of about $2.71 trillion in the United States alone, and nearly $1 out of every $10 under professional management in the United States belonged to socially responsible investment funds like Calvert, Trillium and Portfolio 21. Celent,

that of venture capital have all begun to pressure businesses to factor social, environmental, corporate governance and climate issues into their financial statements, policies, disclosures, credit assessments and lending guidelines. The proper guides for best practices for financial institutions that are dealing with the environment are Equator Principles and the United Nations (UN) Principles for Responsible Investment. Borrowers who want loans from these signatories need to classify and reveal all risks associated with social and environmental performance; they should also provide an alleviation strategy for the management of these risks. The UN Principles for Responsible Investment is another voluntary set of guidelines that provides investors with a range of options for honoring their fiduciary obligations, as well as being aware of the Environmental, Social and Corporate Governance (ESG) issues of the companies of their choice (Wilhelm 2013).

The chapter's objective is to highlight the role of sustainability in business management and pinpoint key factors that determine business success or failure in a sustainable environment. There is a close relation between sustainability and business success. Moreover, problems encountered by companies are important, whether they are economic, social or environmental, and they are crucial for establishing a competitive advantage.

In order to verify the hypotheses and to display the fulfillment of the research's objectives, the following research methods were used: a critical analysis of the literature (related works), observations, case studies and logical reasoning.

We have categorized the sections of the chapter as follows: the first section highlights the trajectory of sustainability; the second section presents the definition of business failure and handles the issue of key business drivers; the third section discusses the role of institutions with regard to the improved allocation of companies' resources; the fourth section raises the problem of human capital and education, and the impact of these factors on companies' resources; and the fifth section deals with environmental issues that relate to negative externalities created while business is being conducted. Finally, the conclusion contains a presentation of final research results.

The Path of Sustainability

The Old Kingdom of ancient Egypt strived to take its civilization into eternity through customs, culture, religion and irrigation technology. Millennia later,

---

a financial consultancy, predicts that the SRI market in the United States will grow beyond $3 trillion within the next few years. These trends are not are not just confined to the United States; as the European SRI market grew by $892 billion in the last two years (Wilhelm, 2013).

and nearly halfway around the world, the Mayans of Central America practiced ecological engineering to conserve water and food, and to preserve a way of life for their descendants. In more recent times, naturalists Ralph Waldo Emerson and Henry David Thoreau in the 1800s and John Muir in the early 1900s championed a close relationship with Earth. Their writings recognized that harmony between man and nature was possible (Higgins 2015).

Many writers, from Plato (*The Republic*) and Sir Thomas More (*Utopia*) onwards have offered sophisticated and detailed visions of future utopian, and sometimes ecotopian, societies. Lewis Mumford produced an enlightening critical study in 1922, *The Story of Utopias*. For those concerned with fashioning a more ecologically sustainable and socially just society, the anarchist ideas of William Morris (*News from Nowhere*), the futurist musings of Edward Bellamy's *Looking Forward* and, more recently, the bioregionalist extrapolations of Ernest Callenbach (*Ecotopia*) are possibly the most interesting and influential. There are also many green apocalyptic science fiction novels, such as John Brunner's *Stand on Zanzibar*, Octavia Butler's *Parable of the Sower* and Geoff Ryman's *Child Garden*, which increasingly are becoming less like fiction and more like the world we inhabit, but it has been those panoramic visions of a future designed for clean, efficient living (Blewitt 2015).

Also, Hanns Carl von Carlowitz in *Sylvicultura oeconomica*, a handbook published in 1713, deals with the question of how to achieve such conservation and cultivation of timber that there would be a *continuous, steady and sustained use*. All of these acts and actions contained a number of practical and interesting proposals with respect to sustainability, which was very useful in the following periods (Grober 2007).

Therefore, the early concept of sustainability has a great historical tradition. In the year 2000, Millennium Development Goals (MDGs) were established and included eight anti-poverty targets to be reached by 2015. Also, the Rio+20 outcome document, *The Future We Want*, called for further mainstream sustainable development at all levels (UN 2012). Since Rio+20 did not propose a clear and measurable goals, and the MDGs were not fully effective, 2015 was to be the year when countries had shaped and adopted a new development agenda that would build on the Millennium Development Goals[2] and would succeed them. In September 2015, the General Assembly of the UN

---

2   The business liturgy accords an important place to resonant assertions of the vital role of production. There are many paroles in this context. *Only the productive can be strong. Only the strong can be free. Production made America [...] Let us stop bickering and produce* (Galbraith, 1998). The Millennium Development Goals were a very useful set of objectives. But there was something missing from these goals as stated: the goal of higher productivity growth. This is an ambitious goal. But seriously addressing global poverty demands nothing less. Empirical studies confirm this (Taylor, 2003).

adopted a new set of 17 Sustainable Development Goals and 169 targets for people, planet and prosperity. The new goals and targets came into effect on January 1, 2016 to guide the decisions we would take over the next 15 years, until 2030 (UN 2015).

In the meantime, the World Bank Group and the Zicklin Center for Business Ethics Research at the Wharton School of the University of Pennsylvania started a very important and ambitious global initiative for young people around the world, under the name *Ideas for Action* (I4A) (Mohieldin and Petkoski, 2015). The people are at the epicenter of sustainable development, and they commit to work together to promote sustained and inclusive economic growth, social development and environmental protection, thereby to benefit all (UN, 2012).

Key Drivers for Business Success and Business Failure

Business failure is a constant part of the contemporary economy, and its importance increases, especially after the crisis that occurred in 2008 (Ucbasaran, Shepherd, Lockett and Lyon 2013). Business failure is a term that has a different meaning and is described in the literature in very different ways. For instance, Pretorius (2009) tackles the definition of business failure and states that it is a huge theoretical challenge to present a unique definition of the concept. According to Shepherd (2005), the lack of a single definition of failure is partly responsible for the poor understanding of the phenomenon. Also, other authors pointed out that there are many different terminologies and taxonomies that are very often mistaken for and related to business failure, but they do not mean exactly the same thing, such as firm closures, entrepreneurial exit, dissolution, discontinuance, insolvency, organizational mortality and bankruptcy, decline and turnaround (Arasti, 2011; Pretorius 2009).

Based on related work, business failure is usually a phenomenon of a financial nature and, in this context, it is defined as wanting or needing to sell or liquidate, to avoid losses or to pay off creditors, or the general inability to make a profitable go of the business (Gaskill et al. 1993; Arasti, 2011). In a more strategic way, the concept of business failure is the termination of a venture that has fallen short of its owner's goals (McGrath, 1999; Ucbasaran et al., 2010).

Further, Pretorius (2009) categorizes business failure definitions in three groups, as can be seen below: decline, failure and turnaround focused and, based on these, he provides the comprehensive, personal definition of business failure: a venture fails when it involuntarily becomes unable to attract new debt or equity funding to reverse decline; consequently, it cannot continue to operate under the current ownership and management. Failure is the endpoint at discontinuance (bankruptcy), and when it is reached, operations cease and judicial proceedings take effect.

Most authors present the definition of business failure in a very restricted way, especially when taking into consideration the prediction of the phenomenon or its aftermath (Altman, 1968; Mantere et al., 2013; Bruton, Khavul and Chavez, 2011). There are also authors such as Deakin (1972) and Chen and Williams (1999), who do not provide a definition of business failure. On the contrary, Dias and Teixeira (2014) have a definition that covers the wide scope of the problem, while tackling the financial and nonfinancial aspects of the concept, and describing business failure, as business closure, either for financially related reasons or willingly, which in the latter case can be due to the owners not achieving their expectations (e.g., not enough current return, no growth expectation, poor performance, etc.) in contrast to personal reasons (e.g., retirement, relocation, family issues, etc.).

Business failure is very often analyzed and associated with business success and is pointed out as the crucial factor that enables entrepreneurs to succeed and grow after the failure (Dias and Teixeira, 2014). Also, the aspect of learning from the experience is an important research field in business failure and business success scope (Cope, 2011). However, there is still little evidence that business failure is a direct key driver in creating platforms for business success.

According to the report, entitled *Evaluation Methodology: Measurement of Drivers of Business Success and Failure* (BIS 2010), there is a difference in the approach and classification of business failure drivers, which are divided into variety of groups. The main typology of factors is based on variety of theoretical perspectives on firm performance. For example: the neoclassical perspective (considers nature and degree of competition in product markets); the resource-based view (financial and physical capital, and human resources); evolutionary models of the firm (the role of innovation, institutions and networks in influencing a firm's progress). The second approach to the drivers' classification pays attention to a leading role of internal and external clusters of determinants, such as: internal, innovation, market diversification, management practices, firm size, firm age, change of ownership, internationalization; and the external group: alliances, networks, location, product market structure, product market and labor market regulations (BIS 2010). The detailed list of key drivers responsible for business failure, developed by Pretorius (2009) is presented in Table 4.1.[3]

---

3 Specifically, Pretorius (2009) distinguishes also moderators who have an impact on the effects of drivers and, among them: the life-cycle stage; the qualitative versus quantitative nature of causes and preconditions related to decline, the age and size effect and the stakeholder perspective.

Table 4.1 List of key drivers developed by Pretorius

No.	Key driver	Author
1	Resource munificence (abundance or absence of resources for the venture)	Castrogiovanni, 1991
2	Resource slack (organization capital); unabsorbed resource slack means increased ability to borrow funds and the ability to generate cash by the company	Levinthal, 1991; Barker & Moné, 1998
3	Negative changing organizational capital; management human capital; reputational slack;	Levinthal, 1991; Barker, Patterson & Mueller 2001; Cressy 2006
4	Environmental munificence (capacity to accommodate firms)	Francis & Desai, 2005
5	Leadership (typically subject to heuristics and biases of management through overconfidence, escalation of commitment bias, risk perception and misconceptions)	Chowdhury & Lang, 1993, citing Boyle & Desai, 1991; Edmunds, 1979, McGuire, 1976; Longenecker, Simoneti & Sharkey, 1999; Le Roux, Pretorius & Millard, 2006; Shepherd 2005
6	Causality (strategic vs. operational origin)	Pearce & Robbins, 1993; Barker & Duhaime, 1997
No.	**Peripheral driver**	**Author**
7	Unique and non-static preconditions (sets of circumstances underlying the decline situation; determine the severity and suddenness of decline and turnaround activities)	Bruton, Ahlstrom & Wan, 2003; Smith & Graves, 2005
8	Extremes dichotomy (assumes that decline is mostly associated with firms experiencing extreme configurations of factors rather than balanced configurations	Probst and Raisch, 2005

Source: Author's elaboration based on Pretorius (2009).

However, this is not the complete list. The extended list of determinants of business success and business failure is presented in Table 4.2.

Based on the Euler Hermes report on the global bankruptcy, three hundred thousand companies went bankrupt in the year 2015 (EH, 2015) and 2016 may indicate a reduction in the number of bankruptcies in North America (2%) and Western Europe (5%), with an increase in the number of bankruptcies in

Table 4.2 Extended list of determinants of business success and failure

Business success companies	Business failure companies
• Effective communications systems	• Believe business is a business
• Are action biased (willingness to try things and experiment)	• Believe all you have to do to increase quality is start inspection programs
• Are quality driven	• Believe big is better
• Are test marketers supreme	• Believe if they just find right
• Are value driven	incentive, productivity will increase
• Audit company's performance quarterly	• Believe in making appearances look good no matter what the truth
• Believe in being decisive	• Believe it's all over if the company
• Believe in being the best	stops growing
• Believe in details	• Easily become content
• Believe in productivity through people not things	• Fear change
• Believe leaders are servants of the people	• Have difficulty delegating
	• Have poor interpersonal skills
• Concentrate on long-term goals not short-term profits	• Lack experience
• De-bureaucratize	• Like power
• Develop new product lines when appropriate	• Like to analyze everything
	• Like to appear mysterious and untouchable
• Encourage innovative thinking	• Like to control everything
• Enjoy their prosperity but never take it for granted	• Like to stick to their plans no matter what the consequences
• Get close to their customers	• Tend to adopt interpersonal, almost passive attitudes to company goals
• Have a profound sense of dissatisfaction with their accomplishments	• Borrow more money than they should
• Have a simple form with lean staff	• Buy more inventories than they can afford to carry
• Have routine and preventative maintenance programs	• Buy too much, too little or the wrong kind of equipment
• Innovate all aspects of their business	• Cater to the wrong kind of client
• Know how to create value of nothing	• Charge too little for their product or services
• Know what business they are really in	• Don't make the effort to develop a loyal customer base
• Listen to people in the trenches	• Don't patch up differences between partners or employers
• Manage to be highly unified and free at the same time	• Don't really understand their customers' needs
• Organize around teams	• Don't seek advice when they need it
• Plan for the future	• Don't take the time to write good business plan
• Regularly update their business plan	
• Reinvest their returns for compounded growth	• Fail to adapt to sudden changes in the marketplace
• Sell benefits not products	• Fail to adequately train their staff

(continued)

Table 4.2 (*cont.*)

Business success companies	Business failure companies
• Start with well-defined distinctive competence	• Fail to check credit references on new customers
• Stick to their area of expertise	• Fail to follow up the overdue accounts
• Structure themselves appropriately	• Fail to include taxes and insurance premiums payable in their profit projections
	• Fail to project cashflow needs
	• Fail to safeguard against unforeseen variables
	• Hire relatives or friends
	• Lack commitment
	• Lack financial feedback systems
	• Lack profits
	• Lack sufficient startup capital
	• Let expenses and costs get out of hand
	• Lose their market share
	• Never know when to quit
	• Overspecialize
	• Overspend
	• Overextend their operations and find it difficult to consolidate
	• Overstaff
	• Pay more taxes than they should
	• Put the fate of their business in the hands of one or two clients
	• Start to take their customers for granted
	• Try to be all things to all people
	• Try to reinvent the wheel
	• Understaff
	• Undertake risky financial alliances

Source: Author's elaborations, based on *Learning Why Companies Succeed and Why They Fail*. The Entrepreneur's Guidebook Series, Patsula Media 2001, pp. 1–46.

Latin America (+14%) and Asia–Pacific (+10%). Additionally, according to Scott Shane, the analysis based on the choice of industry matters a great deal for business success. The researcher plotted five-year survival rates by industry for firms founded in 2005 (Table 4.3).

It is important to note that there is no single list of reasons for business success or business failure. Many authors tackle several factors and put stress on different fields of activity or determinants, internal or external origin. However, in most of the studies, the determinants representing the five capital

Table 4.3 Five-year survival rate (%) according to industry

Industry	5-Year survival rate (%)
Mining	51.3
Manufacturing	48.4
Services	47.6
Wholesaling	47.4
Agriculture	47.4
Retailing	41.1
Finance/Insurance/Real estate	39.6
Transportation	39.4
Communications/Utilities	39.4
Construction	36.4

Source: Gary Brownlee, Small Business Failure Rates and Causes, http://www.isbdc. org/small-business-failure-rates-causes/ and Smallbiztrends.com (accessed June 20, 2016).

models (financial capital, nature capital, human capital, social capital and physical capital) are very often mentioned. These five capitals represent and cover three pillars of sustainability: economic, social and environmental. Concretely, Shadir and Lussier, in their research carried out for Pakistan (2016) summaries that business planning, proper employee staffing, adequate capital inflows and partnerships are important for the viability and success of small businesses. From this perspective, staff (human capital), capital income (financial capital) and social capital matter. On the other hand, Hall and Sobel (2006) analyzed the interactions between public policy and entrepreneurship and pointed out that institutional quality and economic freedom matter for entrepreneurship.

Institutions and Entrepreneurship versus Growth and Development: Why Do They Matter?

From historical and logical perspectives, there are two types of institutions. *Economic institutions* determine the incentives of, and the constraints on, economic actors and shape economic outcomes and society; in particular, they influence investments in physical and human capital and technology, and the organization of production. *Political institutions* allocate de jure political power, while groups with greater economic might typically possess greater de facto political power.[4] Desirable institutions provide security of property rights,

---

4   Interestingly, Montesquieu claimed and argued that despotism would be the political system in warm climates (Acemoğlu, Johnson and Robinson, 2005).

enforce contracts, stimulate entrepreneurship, foster integration in the world economy, maintain macroeconomic stability, manage risk-taking by financial intermediaries, supply social insurance and safety nets. Governments can learn a lot by looking at what works and does not work in other settings (Rodrik 2008).

It is necessary to paint a gloomy picture of the institutional anatomy. Property rights and contract enforcement are two crucial elements of the institutional framework (Beck and Laeven, 2006). Property rights are an instrument of society and derive their significance from the fact that they help one form those expectations which one can reasonably hold in dealings with others. It is clear, then, that property rights specify how persons may be benefited and harmed and, therefore, who must pay whom to modify the actions taken by persons (Demsetz, 1967). Spectacularly, Locke, Smith and Hayek,[5] among many others, emphasized the importance of property rights for the success of nations. Their deprivation could drastically change the environment negatively (Acemoğlu, Johnson and Robinson, 2002). Modern anthropology literature confirms the fact that "private property appears very definitely on primitive levels[6] and that the roots of property as a legal principle which determines the physical relationships between man and his environmental setting, natural and artificial, are the very prerequisite of any ordered action in the cultural sense" (Hayek 1960). Knack and Keefer (1995) found that property rights have a greater impact on investment and growth.

In countries with more secure property rights, firms might better allocate resources and consequentially grow faster as the returns on various types of assets are more protected against competitors' actions. Using data on sectoral value-added for a large number of countries, Claessens and Laeven (2003)

---

5   The recognition of private or several properties is an essential condition for the prevention of coercion, though by no means the only one. We are rarely in a position to carry out a coherent plan of action unless we are certain of our exclusive control of some material objects; and where we do not control them, it is necessary that we know who does if we are to collaborate with others. The recognition of property is clearly the first step in the delimitation of the private sphere which protects us against coercion; and it has long been recognized that "a people averse to the institution of private property is without the first element of freedom and that nobody is at liberty to attack several properties and to say at the same time that he values civilization." In modern society, the property should be sufficiently dispersed, so that the individuals are not dependent on particular persons who alone can provide him or her with what is needed or who alone can employ them. The rules of property and contract are required to delimit the individual's private sphere wherever the resources or services needed for the pursuit of one's aims are scarce and must, in consequence, be under the control of some person or another (Hayek, 1960).

6   For detailed information, see in Veblen (1899/1973).

found very robust evidence consistent with better property rights leading to higher growth through improved asset allocation. Also, Beck and Laeven (2006)[7] indicate a strong and robust relationship between the exogenous component of institutional development and economic growth over the period 1992 to 2004.

Entrepreneurs have higher incentives to work in the formal economy as opposed to the informal economy, if their property rights are protected and contract enforcement allows them to broaden their market outreach (Beck, 2010). The basic functions of government in almost all economic analysis are to protect property from expropriation, to enforce contracts and to resolve disputes. Institutions differ tremendously among capitalist economies. Identifying the appropriate institutions and designing politically feasible reform strategies for introducing them are both the challenge and the hope of the new comparative economics (Djankov, La Porta, Lopez-de-Silanes and Shleifer, 2003).

Education and Human Capital for Business as a Key Element of the Social Pillar of Sustainability

In general, formal schooling is a public good and is funded primarily by the state. Even a well-functioning market economy is not likely to invest enough in education without government subsidies (Pissarides, 2000). Moreover, highly educated workers have a comparative advantage with respect to the adjustment to and implementation of new technologies. This may also have a bearing on the role of government education policy in promoting economic growth. In particular, government subsidies and other policies, which tend to encourage the acquisition of education and increase the relative supply of highly educated workers, will be expected to accelerate the rate of diffusion of new industrial technologies by lowering the costs of adjustment and implementation[8] (Bartel and Lichtenberg, 1987). The effect of education and related investment in individuals is to help them overcome the restraints that are imposed by their environment (Galbraith, 1998).

---

7 Interestingly, authors documented that macroeconomic policies and the speed of reform do not explain the differences in GDP per capita growth across transition economies.

8 Educated persons not only acquire productive skills, but they learn how to learn, which enables them to deal with a changing environment. Being able to understand technology and the production process, moreover, makes them good innovators. There is, therefore, some agreement that average human capital in a society has a positive effect on productivity growth and the implementation of new technologies. The reverse causality is, however, also likely to be of relevance (Kaas and Zink, 2007).

From the foregoing, we can conclude that education has direct and indirect effects on national output. Educated workers raise national income directly because schooling raises their marginal productivity. They raise national income indirectly by increasing the marginal productivity of physical capital and of other workers. In highly educated countries the spillover effect on other workers is minimal, but in less-educated countries it appears to be much larger (Breton, 2013a).

In the first place, it is of vital importance to note that schooling can be considered as a very important determinant of human capital improvement. Average schooling attainment has greater statistical significance to GDP per capita than average test scores (Breton, 2011). In addition, it is important to note that investment in human capital has large external effects on national income, and that these effects are larger in countries with lower levels of human capital (Breton, 2013). Notably, Mankiw, Romer and Weil (1990) narrowed the focus only on human capital investment in the form of education (ignoring investment in health, among other things).

Importantly, one of the earliest questions following the human capital revolution[9] in economic thought was: "If education is a form of capital, what is the rate of return to it?"[10] This led to a related question: "How does the profitability of investment in education compare to investment in physical capital?" Primary schooling remains the number-one priority for investment. The social rate of return to primary education exceeds by several percentage points the

---

9 Human capital theory, originally developed by Theodore Schultz and Gary Becker in the 1960s, shows that the education system has powerful implications for the economy. As far as growth theory is concerned, the main contribution of human capital theory has been to point to investments in human capital as essential to improve long-run macroeconomic performance. Such investment can come from different sources—for example, health, experience, training—but the main focus of human capital theory is education. Education is considered a key driver of growth, given it is a main source of human capital. Economic growth, especially in contemporary knowledge-based economies, results mainly from new ideas, translated into technological innovation (Amaral and Simões, 2015).

10 In a broader sense, it seems plausible that the productive value of education has its roots in two distinct phenomena. Increased education simply may permit a worker to accomplish more with the resources at hand. This *worker effect* is the marginal product of education as marginal product is normally defined, that is, it is the increased output per unit change in education holding other factor quantities constant. On the other hand, increased education may enhance a worker's ability to acquire and decode information about costs and productive characteristics of other inputs. As such, a change in education results in a change in other inputs including, perhaps, the use of some *new* factors that otherwise would not be used. The return to education is therefore considered as consisting of two effects: a *worker effect* and an *allocative effect* (Welch, 1970).

returns to secondary and higher education (Psacharopoulos, 1985). From an economic perspective, a key question is how higher education contributes to social welfare (Miller, 2015).

Like the Roman god Janus, education has two faces. We will observe this hottest subject at the two levels. At the microeconomic level, labor economists find a positive relationship between educational attainment and wages. The human capital theory argues that time spent in school increases wages by directly increasing a worker's productivity level. Alternatively, while acknowledging the direct productivity effects, signaling or screening theories argue that education acts as a screen or filter for productivity differences across workers that are not observable by firms.[11] Therefore, by signaling greater innate productivity, workers with more educational attainment are paid higher wages. Another finding in the labor literature is the *sheepskin* effect[12] (Yamarik and King, 2001). Students will take these hiring criteria into account when deciding how long to stay in school. They will choose a length of schooling to *signal* their ability to employers, and employers will demand a minimum level of schooling from applicants in order to *screen* their workers. Both *signaling* and *screening* serve to *sort* workers according to their unobserved abilities (Weiss, 1995). Screening theories of education suggest that in addition to increasing individual productivity, education serves as a signal of greater productivity, and that this signal is rewarded in the labor market. In sum, while authors are

---

11 The conventional view among economists is that education adds to an individual's productivity and therefore increases the market value of his labor. From the viewpoint of formal theory, it does not matter how the student's productivity is increased, but implicitly it is assumed that the student receives cognitive skills through his education. On contrary, Arrow (1973) presented a very different view. Higher education, in his model, contributes in no way to superior economic performance; it increases neither cognition nor socialization. Instead, higher education serves as a screening device, in that it sorts out individuals of differing abilities, thereby conveying information to the purchasers of labor. The screening or filter theory of higher education is distinct from the productivity-adding human capital theory but is not in total contradiction to it. From the viewpoint of an employer, an individual certified to be more valuable is more valuable to an extent which depends upon the nature of the production function. Therefore, the filtering role of education is a productivity-adding role from the private viewpoint; but as we shall see, the social productivity of higher education is more problematic. The filter theory of education is part of a larger view about the nature of the economic system and its equilibrium. It is based on the assumption that economic agents have highly imperfect information. In particular, the purchaser of a worker's services has a very poor idea of his productivity. In this model, it is assumed instead that the buyer has very good statistical information but nothing more.

12 Sheepskin effects are discrete increases in the return to education that arises after completing a degree (Heckman, Layne-Farrar and Todd, 1996).

reluctant to interpret the results as purely causal effects of diploma receipt on wages, they suggest that sheepskin effects[13] do matter in the returns to education (Jaeger and Page, 1996).

The Third Pillar of Sustainability: Environmental Issues versus Business

The views about development and sustainability issues have evolved over the years. Economists are always preoccupied with maximizing economic activity. The natural environment plays an important role in supporting economic growth prospects. Natural resources are, therefore, vital for securing economic growth and development, not just today, but for future generations. Before describing the intricacies, it is useful to mention that the notion and tangential concern for sustainability and environment among the economists has a long history, dating back to 1848 and John Stuart Mill's famous chapter *Of the Stationary State*, a situation that Mill, unlike other classical economists, welcomed (Ekins, 2000; Daly, 2007). Also, the great English economist Alfred Marshall was able to write on the title page of his *Principles of Economics*, first published in 1890, "*natura non facit saltum* (nature makes no leaps)" (Cypher and Dietz, 2009). Hence, sustainability is not a new idea in economics,[14] instead, it is embedded in the very concept of income by Sir John Hicks and Irving Fisher. As defined by Hicks, income is the maximum that can be consumed in a given year without reducing the capacity to produce and consume the same amount next year. By definition, income is sustainable consumption (Daly, 2007). The practical purpose of income is to serve as a guide for prudent conduct (Hicks, 1946). In *The Nature of Capital and Income* (1906), Fisher argued that *income* is the enjoyable flow of services from capital and human beings. He provided the original insight that the most complete measure of current wealth should be the present value of future consumption (Brennan, 2009; Hamilton, 2010).

In 1972, at the United Nations Conference on the Human Environment in Stockholm, the Club of Rome (Meadows et al., 1972) initiated the first serious international discussion of global environmental issues (Blewitt, 2015). The Meadows report showed the possibility of poisoning of the world population unless an anti-pollution policy was added to the conventional set of policy

---

13 Jaeger and Page (1996) find little evidence that the sheepskin effects of high school and college graduation differ across race and sex groups.

14 Using modem terminology, we might say that the economists such as David Ricardo, Alfred Marshall, Arthur Pigou or Harold Hotelling made significant contributions to the subject of sustainable development (Sterner, 1994).

instruments. An intensive international discussion ensued about the various forms in which pollution can occur, such as acid rain threatening the world's forests, the pollution of the atmosphere by the smoke of factories and by the gases emitted by automobiles, and so forth. The generally accepted directive is that *the polluter must pay*. This is meant to say that it is not the general public that should finance anti-pollution policy, but rather the producers and hence the consumers of the specific goods and services causing pollution (Tinbergen, 1994). Jan Tinbergen states that two things are unlimited reservoirs: "the number of generations we should feel responsible for and our inventiveness."

The sustainable development paradigm is based on an economic, not ecological, rationality. Discourses of sustainable development embody a view of nature specified by modern economic thought (Banerjee, 2003). For instance, Holtz-Eakin and Selden (1992) examined the relationship between economic development and emissions of carbon dioxide, a greenhouse gas central to global warming predictions. Estimates derived from global panel data suggest a diminishing marginal propensity to emit (MPE) carbon dioxide (CO_2) as GDP per capita rises. Moreover, the sensitivity analyses suggest that the overall pace of economic development does not dramatically alter the future annual or cumulative flow of CO_2 emissions. Whether productive capacity should be transmitted across generations in the form of mineral deposits or capital equipment or technological knowledge is more a matter of efficiency than of equity (Solow, 1986).

In this sense and logic, sustainability is fundamentally and basically a matter of renewable resources. When nonrenewable resources are used, they automatically and by default become unavailable to future generations. The rule to follow here is to use them at the correct rate, *neither too fast nor too slow*, and to see to it that the natural wealth they represent is converted into long-lived, human-made wealth as they are used. Thus, for example, the mineral resources of many developing countries must be converted to long-term productive capital, both private and public, if they are to contribute to the long-run economic development of the extracting country. By productive capital we mean not only physical capital (roads, factories, etc.), but also human capital (education, skills) and what we might call institutional capital (an efficient legal system, effective public agencies, etc.) (Field and Field, 2016). In the short term, sustainability is more concerned with a *feasible* rather than a *desirable society* (Curzio, Fortis, Zoboli, 1994).

Furthermore, the old static economic model has been behind many dire predictions of economic disaster and human catastrophe. Moreover, the static mindset that environmentalism is inevitably costly has created a self-fulfilling gridlock, whereby both regulators and industry battle over every inch of territory. On the contrary, some authors believe that the properly designed environmental standards can trigger innovation that may partially, or more than fully, offset the costs of complying with them. It is sometimes argued that companies must, by the very notion of profit seeking, be pursuing all profitable innovations.

Conclusion

Factors defining and impacting business success and business failure evolve and differ over the years, and according to sectors and companies. In terms of sustainability, the operational success of a business means not only generating profit and increasing the value of the company, but also the ability to maintain balance between the three pillars of sustainability and consumption and absorption of five capitals in such a way that the next generation will also benefit from common resources and capital in the same way.

Being successful in business means that one should use resources in a responsible way and earn profits at the same time. A socially responsible and successful business is not easy to run and more costly than traditional businesses because several rules need to be observed, as well as procedures and strategies regarding the public policy, since the shaping of a framework for such a business is extremely important. That is why efficient public policies and institutions of all kinds play a crucial role in the implementation of sustainability in business. Sustainability is a must in contemporary business, and may be a success and failure factor simultaneously. Socially responsible investors and companies should have priorities in public policy, and consumer choices in such companies reduce the risk of future business failure.

Reasonable absorption of limited and rare resources by socially responsible business results in securing access to rare resources in the future, so the companies that absorb natural resources in their activity will have little or no trouble with accessing those resources and continuing production in the future. Also, effective management of human capital means higher productivity. Therefore, we can conclude that sustainability pays off, and it is a key factor in creating the strategy for business success, or for those companies that do not follow sustainability rules and will most probably encounter business failure.

References

Acemoğlu, D., Johnson, S. and Robinson, J. A. (2002). "Reversal of fortune: Geography and institutions in the making of the modern world income distribution." *Quarterly Journal of Economics* 117(4): 1231–94.

Altman, E. I. (1968). "Financial ratios, discriminant analysis and the prediction of corporate bankruptcy." *The Journal of Finance* 23(4): 589–609.

Arasti, Z. (2011). "An empirical study on the causes of business failure in Iranian context," *African Journal of Business Management* 5(17): 7488–98.

Banerjee, S. B. (2003). "Who sustains whose development? Sustainable development and the reinvention of nature." *Organization Studies* 24(1): 143–80.

Bartel, A. P. and Lichtenberg, F. R. (1987). "The comparative advantage of educated workers in implementing new technology." *The Review of Economics and Statistics*, 69(1): 1–11.

Beck, T. and Laeven, L. (2006). "Institution building and growth in transition economies." *Journal of Economic Growth*, 11(2): 157–86

Beck, T. H. L. (2010). Legal institutions and economic development. Discussion Paper No. 2010–94, Center for Economic Research, Tilburg University.

Bewley H., Forth J. and Robinson C. (2010). *Evaluation Methodology: Measurement of Drivers of Business Success and Failure*, BIS, Department of Business Innovation & Skill: 1–92.

Blewitt, J. (2015). *Understanding Sustainable Development*. 2nd edn. New York and London: Routledge.

Brennan, A. J. (2009). Measures of environmental and sustainable socioeconomic welfare and the political economy of capitalism—theoretical reconstruction, technical specification, and critical analysis. GDP, ISEW and GPI. PhD dissertation, Global Political Economy Research Unit, Department of Economics and Finance, Curtin University.

Breton, T. R. (2011). "The quality vs. the quantity of schooling: What drives economic growth?" *Economics of Education Review* 30(4): 765–73.

Breton, T. R. (2013). "The role of education in economic growth: Theory, history and current returns." *Educational Research* 55(2): 121–38.

Breton, T. R. (2013a). "Were Mankiw, Romer, and Weil right? A reconciliation of the micro and macro effects of schooling on income." *Macroeconomic Dynamics* 17(5): 1023–54.

Bruton, G. D., Khavul, S. and Chavez, H. (2011). "Microlending in emerging economies: Building a new line of inquiry from the ground up". *Journal of International Business Studies* 42(5): 718–39.

Business Insolvency Worldwide (2015). Economic Outlook no. 1220–1221, Euler Hermes Economic Research, Paris, September–October.

Chen, J. H. and Williams, M. (1999). "The determinants of business failures in the US low technology and high-technology industries." *Applied Economics* 31(12): 1551–63.

Claessens, S. and Laeven, L. (2003). "Financial development, property rights, and growth." *The Journal of Finance* 58(6): 2401–36.

Cope, J. (2011). "Entrepreneurial learning from failure—an interpretative phenomenological analysis." *Journal of Business Venturing* 26(6): 604–23.

Curzio, A. Q., Fortis, M. and Zoboli, R. "Innovation, resources and economic growth: Changing interactions in the world economy." In A. Q. Curzio, M. Fortis and R. Zoboli, eds. (1994). *Innovation, Resources and Economic Growth* (pp. 3–35). Berlin and Heidelberg: Springer-Verlag.

Cypher, J. M. and Dietz, J. L. (2009). *The Process of Economic Development*. 3rd edn. London and New York: Routledge.

Daly, H. E. (2007). *Ecological Economics and Sustainable Development: Selected Essays of Herman Daly*. Advances in Ecological Economics. Cheltenham and Northampton, MA: Edward Elgar Publishing.

Deakin, E. B. (1972). "A discriminant analysis of predictors of business failure. *Journal of Accounting Research* 10(1): 67–179.

Demsetz, H. (1967). "Toward a theory of property rights." *The American Economic Review* 57(2): 347–59.

Dias, A. R. and Teixeira, A. A. C. (2014). *The Anatomy of Business Failure: A Qualitative Account of its Implications for Future Business Success.* FEP Working Papers, no. 550: 1–25.

Djankov, S., La Porta, R., Lopez-de-Silanes, F. and Shleifer, A. (2003). "Appropriate institutions." In B. Pleskovic and N. Stern, eds. *The New Reform Agenda* (pp. 283–301). Annual World Bank Conference on Development Economics. Washington, DC, and New York: World Bank and Oxford University Press.

Ekins, P. (2000). *Economic Growth and Environmental Sustainability: The Prospects for Green Growth.* London and New York: Routledge.

Emerson, J. (2003). "The blended value proposition: Integrating social and financial returns." *California Management Review* 45(4): 35–51.

Field, B. C. and Field, M. K. (2016). *Environmental Economics: An Introduction.* New York: McGraw-Hill.

Galbraith, J. K. (1998). *The Affluent Society.* Fortieth Anniversary Edition. Boston and New York: Houghton Mifflin Company.

Grober, U. (2007). "Deep roots: A conceptual history of 'sustainable development' (Nachhaltigkeit)." WZB Discussion Paper, no. P 2007-002.

Hall, J. C. and Sobel, R. S. (2006). *Public Policy and Entrepreneurship.* Centre for Applied Economics, University of Kansas. Technical Report 06-0717: 1–24, https://business. ku.edu/sites/businessdev.drupal.ku.edu/files/images/general/Research/TR%2006-0717--Entrepreneur%20(Hall%20%26%20Sobel).pdf (accessed June 20, 2016.

Hayek, F. A. (1960). *The Constitution of Liberty.* Chicago: University of Chicago Press.

Hicks, J. R. (1946). *Value and Capital.* 2nd edn. Oxford: Clarendon Press.

Higgins, K. L. (2015). *Economic Growth and Sustainability Systems Thinking for a Complex World.* San Diego, London and Waltham: Elsevier Publishing.

Hyder, S. and Lussier, R. N. (2016). "Why businesses succeed or fail: A study on small businesses in Pakistan." *Journal of Entrepreneurship in Emerging Economies* 8(1): 82–100.

Jaeger, D. A. and Page, M. E. (1996). "Degrees matter: New evidence on sheepskin effects in the returns to education." *The Review of Economics and Statistics*, 78(4): 733–39.

Jeucken, M. (2001). *Sustainable Finance and Banking: The Financial Sector and the Future of the Planet.* London: Earthscan Publications.

Knack, S. and Keefer, P. (1997). "Does social capital have an economic payoff? A cross-country investigation." *The Quarterly Journal of Economics* 112(4): 1251–88.

Mantere, A., Aula, P., Schildt, H. and Vaara, E. (2013). "Narrative attributions of entrepreneurial failure." *Journal of Business Venturing* 28(4): 459–73.

Miller, J. B. (2015). Higher education: Should other countries follow the US model? Mimeo.

Mohieldin, M. and Petkoski, Dj. (2015). *Financing Sustainable Development: Ideas for Action.* Washington, DC: International Bank for Reconstruction and Development, Part of The World Bank Group.

Pissarides, C. A. (2000). Human capital and growth: A synthesis report. OECD Development Centre Working Paper no. 168, OECD Publishing, Paris.

Pretorius, M. (2009). "Defining business decline, failure and turnaround: A content analysis." *SAJESBM NS* 2(1): 1–16.

Psacharopoulos, G. and Patrinos, H. A. (2004). "Returns to investment in education: A further update." *Education Economics* 12(2): 111–34.

Rodrik, D. (2008b). "Second-best institutions." *The American Economic Review* 98(2): 100–4.

Shepherd, D. A. (2005). The theoretical basis for my plenary speech about our successes and failures at research on business failure. Proceedings: [Conference on] Regional Frontiers of Entrepreneurial Research. Brisbane. February 123–34.

Solow, R. M. (1996). "On the intergenerational allocation of natural resources." *The Scandinavian Journal of Economics* 88(1): 141–49.

Soppe, A. (2004). "Sustainable corporate finance." *Journal of Business Ethics* 53(1–2): 213–24.

Tinbergen, J. (1994). "International order and natural resources." In A. Q. Curzio, M. Fortis and R. Zoboli, eds. *Innovation, Resources and Economic Growth* (pp. 279–89). Berlin and Heidelberg: Springer-Verlag.

Ucbasaran D., Westhead, P., Wright, M. and Flores, M. (2010). "The nature of entrepreneurial experience, business failure and comparative optimism." *Journal of Business Venturing* 25: 541–55

Ucbasaran, D., Shepherd, D. A., Lockett, A. and Lyon, S. J. (2013). "Life after business failure—the process and consequences of business failure for entrepreneurs." *Journal of Management* 39(1): 163–202.

UN General Assembly (2012). *The Future We Want.* Available at: http://www.uncsd2012.org/thefuturewewant.html.

UN General Assembly (2015). *Transforming Our World: The 2030 Agenda for Sustainable Development.* Available at: https://sustainabledevelopment.un.org/post2015/transformingourworld.

Weiss, A. (1995). "Human capital vs. signaling explanations of wages." *Journal of Economic Perspectives* 9(4): 133–54.

Wilhelm, K. (2013). *Return on Sustainability: How Business Can Increase Profitability and Address Climate Change in an Uncertain Economy.* Upper Saddle River, NJ.

Yamarik, S. and King, R. (2001). *Education and State-Level Economic Growth: Is Productivity a Matter of Degree?* Available at: http://www3.uakron.edu/econ/faculty/yamarik/re-final.pdf.

Chapter 5

IMPLEMENTATION OF THE ENTERPRISE RESOURCE PLANNING SYSTEMS: CASE STUDIES OF FAILURES AND THEIR IMPACT ON THE ENTERPRISE OPERATION

Magdalena Malinowska and Andrzej Rzeczycki

Abstract

In this chapter we discuss the problem of enterprise resource planning (ERP) system implementation failure. Presented here is a short description of the ERP system's complexity and the methodological background of implementation. The statistics concerning the implementations process and their results are gathered. Additionally, the lesson learned from the ERP implementation's failures and guidelines on how to prepare the proper implementation process are given.

Complexity of ERP System—a Brief History

ERP is software often perceived as a backbone for a whole business due to the integration, in one application, of the core aspects of the enterprise function—accounting, finance, HR/payroll, production, sales, logistics, inventory and so forth. The development of ERP has almost a fifty-year history (Figure 5.1): the term was introduced by The Gartner Group in 1990 as a consequence of its application not only in industry but also in non-manufacturing enterprises (Antero, 2015; Jacobs and Weston, 2006).

The origins of ERP date back to the 1970s, when the Materials Requirements Planning (MRP) systems began to be developed by ERP vendors and used to support production processes and inventory control systems

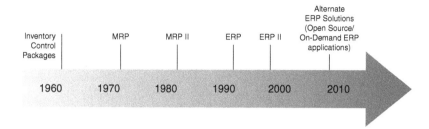

Figure 5.1 The evolution of ERP systems.
Source: Focus Research ERP Group 2009.

(Jacobs and Weston, 2006; Abramek et al. 2014). The crucial element of MRP systems was integration of the inventory processes, material management and production on the basis of a prepared production schedule. In comparison with the previously known inventory control systems, the MRP was equipped with a module responsible for forecasting and determining the range of inventories as well as for tracking and quantitative settlement of production. Three main objectives were the background for developing the MRP system:

1. availability of materials, components and products for production and for client delivery;
2. maintaining the lowest possible materials, components and products in the company;
3. planning manufacturing activities, delivery schedules and purchasing activities.

MRP allowed companies to reduce inventories, define materials and components delivery time, analyze production costs, to make more effective use of the infrastructure, have faster response to changes observed in the environment, control the various production stages, collect the business data for analysis and do better planning.

The progressive development of MRP systems was the background for extension of the concept of operational management for the whole manufacturing process, including such aspects as marketing, finance and sales. Integration of capacity resource planning, production, cost control, sales analysis and forecasting in one system led to the development of Manufacturing Resource Planning (MRP II).

However, the heart of MRP II was MRP, and the new standard extends the advantages of the previous system. Through integration and coordination of the entire manufacturing process, including material, finance, labor and machine capacity, it was possible to implement forecasting functions to predict future demand and, as a consequence, to determine the capacity requirement, plan the level of production, personnel and inventories in the short- and long-term.

Since the 1990s the MRP II has been replaced with ERP systems, which have been become the third stage of integration and advanced functions implementation, applicable for industries beyond manufacturing. ERP systems enable the complex management of the entire enterprise due to integration of the MRP II functionalities with the new ones, including human resource management, quality management, distribution and service, customer relationship management, controlling and financial analysis, project management and reporting. The currently existing ERP systems are even more advanced. They are often perceived as a new generation and named ERP II or even ERP III, because their capabilities not only optimize and support the company's internal processes but also enable collaboration with external vendors and suppliers in terms of supply, design, engineering and so forth, so they can directly impact productivity, cost and efficiency (Abramek et al. 2014; Wood 2010). Modern ERP systems are oriented to learning the customers' needs on the marketplace to create, produce and sell (or distribute) innovative products and services. As described in the literature, the current state of ERP systems and trends of their development underline such aspects of their functioning, such as complexity, integration, distance access and borderless collaboration (Patil et al. 2015; IT Polska News 2014; Abramek 2014; Wood 2010; Møller 2016; Burnson 2016; Computer Profile 2015). On the other hand, technology development allows developers to offer Cloud solutions—Cloud ERP or SaaS (System as a Service). This direction is highly supported by ERP vendors, who offer leading products in this technology.

Implementation of ERP Systems—from the Methodological Background to Value of Failure

ERP system implementation depends on many factors: size and location of the company, range of business processes, clients' requirements concerning the expected goals, selected vendors, complexity of implemented modules, software customization and so forth (IT Polska News 2014).

Unlike the previous few years, the 2016 Panorama Consulting Report indicates that the level of satisfaction from the ERP software increased by 5 percent over the previous year. The statistics show that 74 percent of the report's respondents would select this software again if required to start over (Panorama Consulting 2016).

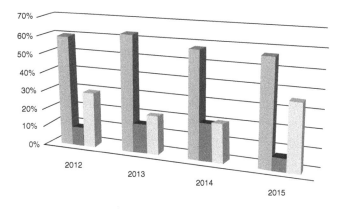

	2012	2013	2014	2015
▦ Success	60%	63%	58%	57%
■ Failure	10%	16%	21%	7%
▨ Neutral or don't know	30%	21%	21%	36%

▦ Success   ■ Failure   ▨ Neutral or don't know

Chart 5.1 Assessment of the ERP implementations' outcome in the years 2012–15. *Source*: Authors' own elaboration based on Panorama Consulting Solutions 2016, 2015, 2014, 2013, 2012.

Interestingly, the surveys show that in 2015 the percentage of those who assessed their implementation outcome as a success decreased by 1 percent in comparison to 2014 and 6 percent in comparison to 2013 (Chart 5.1) (Panorama Consulting Solutions 2016, 2015, 2014, 2013).

However, the huge increase in perceiving the implementation outcome as a failure is noticed (Chart 5.1). The observed decrease in failure is the lowest since 2012, reaching 7 percent. At the same time, the percentage of those who claimed neutrality or responded, "don't know" with regard to project outcomes increased. The achieved result of "don't know" answers was rated at 36 percent in 2015. The reasons this fact might be caused by lack of communication about a project, inadequate time in software selection, not defined or not precisely defined measurement of the implementation benefits and post-implementation audits (Panorama Consulting Solutions 2016).

Despite the fact that failures happened in the implementation of ERP systems, the ERP market is clearly growing. In 2013, it was worth $25.4 billion, higher by 3.8 percent over the previous year. There are many ERP vendors (Chart 5.2), who offer the software suitable for different sizes of companies and different profiles. The unquestioned leader has been SAP, known as the

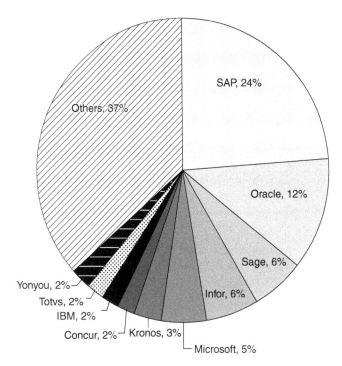

Chart 5.2 Top ERP vendors—ERP market share in 2013.
Source: Columbus, 2014.

first real ERP vendor and, in 2013, held a 24 percent market share. Other significant players include Oracle, who came into the ERP market through acquisition of major ERP systems (JD Edwards and PeopleSoft) as well as Sage, Infor and Microsoft.

Methodology of ERP system implementations

System implementation is a process that includes the software installation, its start-up, adaptation and exploitation. The methodology of implementation presents the detailed characteristic of activities that are undertaken to finalize the implementation process and include the procedures, aims, rules and instruments required to lead the process in an organized way (Lutovac 2012).

The management of ERP implementation requires considering the following (Krupa 2016):

- main processes, which involve, in particular: analysis of the organizational structure of the company and its business processes, data migration, the installation, administration and configuration the function and interfaces, testing, deployment, end user training, post-implementation assist and support,

- auxiliary processes, which involve, in particular: project management, information and motivation policy, quality management, risk management, change management and training.

Many ERP vendors run the implementation using their own methodology, which is based on PMI, PROMET or Prince2. There are also specified methodologies applied by the vendors: Go Forward (BCC), ASAP (SAP) ASAP/SPRINT (7milowy), Microsoft SureStep (Microsoft), ROI5 (Exact), Q-Advantage (DSR), Easy On-Boarding (DSR), Epicor Signature (Epicor), IFS/Implementation (IFS), Infor OPIM (Infor), StepWise (Infor), AIM (Advanced Implementation Methodology—Oracle), OneMethodology (Oracle), SIGMA (Sage Implementation Global Methodology Approach—Sage), Target Enterprise (BaaN) (IT Polska News 2014; Lutovac 2012; Salimi 2005).

One of the well-known methodologies is ASAP (Accelerated SAP). ASAP is a step-by-step guide to implement SAP, which evolved by the years of experience of SAP ERP (earlier SAP R/3) implementations (SAP 2016; Kalaimani 2016; Krupa 2016). The methodology consists of six phases (Table 5.1), which are supported by the following set of tools:

- Project Estimator—to enable the consultants' smooth and precise identification of resources, cost and time frame of implementation; it takes into account the project scope and risk factors;
- Concept Check Tool—for quality control of the project elaboration, technical infrastructure and software configuration settings; it allows for informing about potential data volume and configuration conflicts that could lead to performance issues if not addressed,
- Implementation Assistant (IMG)—to navigate the activities/tasks during implementation, which are precisely described with "what and how" descriptions; it consists of: (a) the Roadmap with work packages, activities and tasks; (b) the Project Plan with budget plan, resource plan and work plan; (c) the Knowledge Corner with the set of configuration guides, technical documentation and training materials;
- Q&A Database—equipped by a set of questions and answers that were the basis for the business concept of implementation;
- Reference Model—included in the set of business processes elaborated as a best practices solution.

Table 5.1 Phases of ASAP methodology.

Phase	Goal	Main activities	Result
Project preparation	Initial planning and implementation process preparation	– Defining the project goals and objectives – Defining the scope of implementation – Defining the sequence in project that has to be executed – Establishing the working group	– Project strategic framework, – Working documentation, – The initial scope of implementation, – An implementation strategy, – Preliminary end user training strategy – Implementation teams, – Required technical and organizational resources
Blueprint	Archive a common understanding of how the company intends to run SAP to support their business	– "As-is" analysis to understand the business processes – Mapping the business processes in SAP – "to-be" analysis – Gap analysis presenting the business process which can't be mapped into standard SAP	– Business Blueprint (Baseline Build and Project Backlog)—detailed documentation gathered during requirements workshops. It allows to create the organizational and configurational basis for system's implementation and establish the range of the development activities.
Realization	Implement all the business process requirements based on the Business Blueprint	– Baseline configuration (major scope); – Final configuration (remaining scope);	– Multiple releases with number of time-boxed iterations focused on building up the functionality

(continued)

Table 5.1 *(cont.)*

Phase	Goal	Main activities	Result
		– Testing the implemented system, – Development of the required interfaces, extensions, reports, forms, archive system, training materials for end user	– System tested in pre-production environments – Trained staff
Final preparation	Complete the final preparation (including testing, end user training, system management and cutover activities)	– Testing of each module – Integrate testing of modules – User training	
Support	Move from a project-oriented, pre-production environment to live production operation.	– Planning the live production operation – Running the system in live production conditions – Reviewing the benefits of an ongoing basis – Ad hoc supporting	– Properly worked SAP system – Help Desk & Competency Center
Operate	Ensure the operability of the solution	– Monitoring the transaction system and optimizing performance (improving live operations)	– Efficient and properly worked SAP system

Source: Authors' own elaboration based on SAP 2016; Kalaimani 2016; Krupa 2016.

As can be seen, the implementation process in accordance with the ASAP methodology is structured and standardized. A similar situation is observed also in other methodologies, which allows for securing the implementation against disorder and ensuring the ability to easily monitor deliverables and critical success factors. Such an approach is important, because implementation of an ERP system is a huge, strategic and complex project involving considerable risks reflected in the time, scope and cost of project implementation.

However, as mentioned, the statistic 60 percent of ERP projects have failed and even the best methodology is insufficient if people are not prepared for changes, business processes are not properly identified and mapped in the system, the objectives are changed during the implementation, the project plan is not a stable foundation for implementation process or the time frames and budget are missing (Ghosh 2012). In the literature, we can find many examples of ERP failures, which illustrates the fundamental problems and the lesson to be learned from the failures. The short analysis is presented in the next parts of the chapter.

Reasons for the ERP implementation failures

Implementation failure might be perceived in many ways. Frequently, the following reasons are pointed to for the unsuccessful implementation of an ERP system (Ghosh 2012):

- lower returns than expected;
- inability of the ERP system to meet predetermined functional requirements;
- surpassing budget limitations;
- higher maintenance and training costs;
- missing development and deployment dates;
- incorrect working of the system;
- not living up to expectations.

The reasons indicated can be considered in terms of how efficiency is defined. From the point of efficiency's definition, we can talk about ineffective or inefficient implementation (Figure 5.2). Effectiveness is primarily concerned with the implementation of the established functionality and the accompanying organizational changes. These immediately become the reason for the achievement of anticipated profits or other benefits of ERP implementation. The efficiency of the implementation concerns the adherence to established schedules and budgets, as well as the methods of conducting the changes. Changes in the budget and the schedule do not directly affect the achievement of the benefits, but they have an impact on the rate of return on investment.

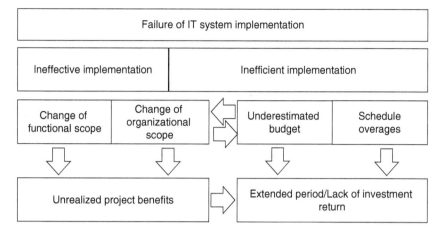

Figure 5.2 Reasons for a failed ERP system implementation.
Source: Authors' own elaboration.

Table 5.2 Performance measures implementation of ERP systems in 2011–15.

Year	Average cost	Cost overruns (%)	Average duration (months)	Duration overruns (%)	Receiving 50% or less benefits (%)
2015	$3.8M	57	21.1	57	46
2014	$4.5M	55	14.3	75	41
2013	$2.8M	54	16.3	72	66
2012	$7.1M	53	17.8	61	60
2011	$10.5M	56	16.0	54	48

Source: Authors' own elaboration based on Panorama Consulting Solutions 2016, 2015, 2014, 2013, 2012.

As the statistics show, ineffective and inefficient implementations are often analyzed, such as in the research carried out by Panorama Consulting for companies engaged in implementation of ERP systems. In 2011–15, such a study was performed for (per annum) 246, 172, 192, 562 and 215 companies implementing ERP systems around the world. The average results encountered during implementation are presented in Table 5.2. In the analyzed period, the average cost of implementation amounted to $5.7 million. Some

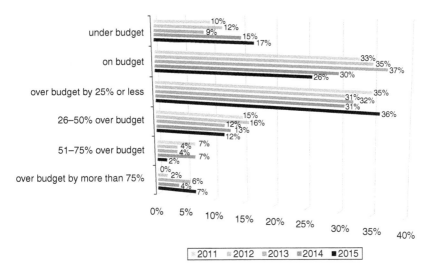

Chart 5.3 Budget execution of ERP implementation in the years 2011–15.
Source: Authors' own elaboration based on Panorama Consulting Solutions 2016, 2015, 2014, 2013, 2012.

55 percent of implementations suffered because of budget overruns. Average scheduled time for implementation was 17.1 months, and for several years the number of implementations exceeding the designated schedule steadily grew. Only in 2015 was there a change in this trend.

Taking a closer view at the scale of underestimated budgets, the last five years (Chart 5.3) can indicate some kind of stagnation of results. Over the years, more than 30 percent of deployments exceeded the budget by 25 percent or less, and 2–7 percent ended up exceeding the budget by more than 75 percent. On average, for 10 percent of companies, implementation ended up costing below budget which, although for companies this is a benefit, from the point of view of the effectiveness of planning it should also be considered as an error of implementation.

In the last few years Panorama's ERP Reports also indicated the reasons for exceeding budgets (Chart 5.4). Among the most frequently indicated were: expanded scope, unanticipated technical/organizational issues and underestimated project staffing. As noted, these reasons are connected firmly with the redesign of processes accompanying the implementation of the ERP system.

The schedule overruns (Chart 5.5) were more volatile than budget overruns. The percent of implementation in line with the schedule in 2011–14

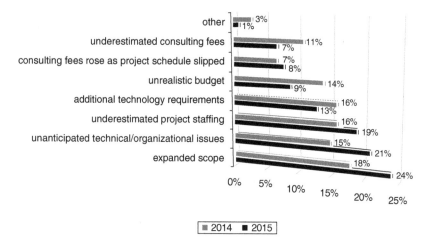

Chart 5.4 Reasons for budget overruns of ERP implementation in the years 2014–15.
Source: Authors' own elaboration based on Panorama Consulting Solutions 2016, 2015.

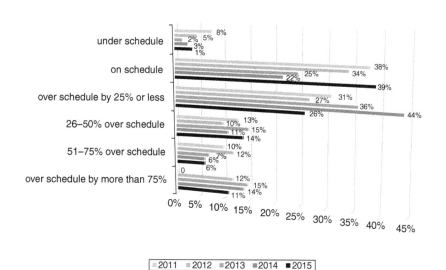

Chart 5.5 Schedule overrun of ERP implementation in the years 2011–15.
Source: Authors' own elaboration based on Panorama Consulting Solutions 2016, 2015, 2014, 2013, 2012.

gradually decreased, but has improved significantly in 2015 and amounted to 39 percent of the responses. In the analyzed period, 11–15 percent of companies exceeded the schedule by more than 75 percent.

In the years 2014–15 the dominant reasons for exceeding the implementation schedule were distinguished (Chart 5.6), which means a considerable

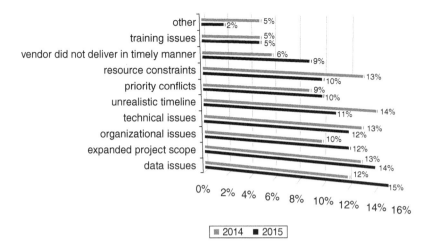

Chart 5.6 Reasons for schedule overruns of ERP implementation in the years 2014–15.
Source: Authors' own elaboration based on Panorama Consulting Solutions 2016, 2015.

diversity of problems. In 2015, compared to 2014, more respondents pointed to time frame issues as the reason for schedule overages. One should not forget that those reasons are interrelated. Organizations that spend the time developing a data migration strategy and plan well before the implementation directory are less likely to experience time frame issues caused by extended durations of implementation.

Some organizations are so overwhelmed by the task of implementation that they overlook the importance of quantifying long-term returns. Fortunately, according to research, fewer and fewer firms do not know their return on investment and have not recovered costs of implementation (Chart 5.7). There is a constant increase in the percentage of enterprises that have recovered costs incurred in a period of less than one year.

Viewed from the prism of collective research, it can therefore be inferred that science flowing from unsuccessful implementations does not have as positive an effect as we might expect. And although it is true that each implementation is different and requires a specialized approach to support elimination of budget and schedule overruns, it is still an impossible task.

Value of the ERP implementations' failure

In the literature, there are many cases of ERP implementation failures. Analysis of their consequences indicates that they had significant meaning for the business (Table 5.3). The observed effects are not only the financial

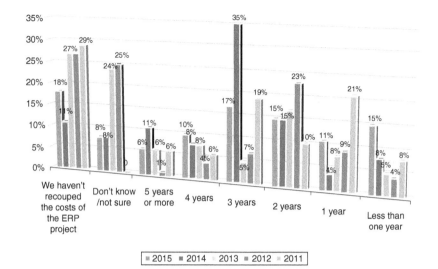

Chart 5.7 Timeline to recoup costs of ERP implementation in the years 2011–15. *Source*: Authors' own elaboration based on Panorama Consulting Solutions 2016, 2015, 2014, 2013, 2012.

problems, losing the trust of customers, organizational conflicts and desta-bilization of organizational structure, but in some cases also bankruptcy or acquisition of the company by an external unit.

All these cases confirm, that ERP implementation is not a simple task. Every implementation requires an appropriate adjustment processes or an IT system, employees' preparation and finding rational management of the pro-ject. Usually, the basic problem is thus the lack of knowledge and understand-ing. Well-established decisions based on knowledge is an important element of efficient implementation and can alleviate perturbations. However, it is crucial for the managers to realize that making decisions cannot be based only on the experience of IT solution providers.

Based on the list in Table 5.3, cases of such implementations can be distin-guished by several basic recommendations for companies:

1. Properly specify needs and match them to the most suitable system.
   Motivation is the key to successful implementation. If a company is not able to determine the aims of system implementation, then it is virtually doomed to failure. However, consultations are necessary, and manag-ers and company owners should remember that the specified needs must have a source in the processes realized in the company and its interactions with the environment. The decision as to whether the system is adapted to

Table 5.3 Famous failed implementations of ERP systems in the past 20 years.

Year	Firm	ERP Provider/ System	Problem	Impact/Result
1996 (started 1993)	Foxmeyer Drug	Andersen Consulting/ SAP R3	New order management and distribution systems didn't work, and fulfillment the cost targets built into contracts were unattainable.	Huge sales losses; Foxmeyer filed for bankruptcy, and has been finally bought by McKesson.
1997	FurnitureCo	SAP R/3	The implemented system could only calculate the costs by using a quota planned a priori. Consequently, there were often huge discrepancies between the reports generated by the ERP system and real-world situation.	The maintenance fee was around $700,000 a year. FurnitureCo decided to switch to a local ERP system—Kingdee's K/3.
1998	ElectricCo	Symix	Changed the company structure during the implementation to adapt to the market; system was not flexible enough to adapt to the sudden organizational change.	Some ERP modules were being used only in a few ElectricCo subsidiary factories; contract for $610,000 ended.
1999 (started 1997)	Hershey Foods	SAP AG, Siebel Systems and Manugistic i2 Technologies	Order management and warehouse implementation issues caused Hershey to miss critical Halloween shipments.	Company said at least $150 million in revenue lost; profit dropped 19%, and stock price went from 57 to 38.
2000	Nike	i2 Technologies	Trouble with new planning system caused inventory and orders woes.	Nike blamed software related issues for $100 million revenue shortfall for the quarter; stock dropped 20%.
2001 (started 1997)	Nestle	SAP AG and Manugistics	Workers didn't understand how to use the new system; they didn't even understand the new processes.	Company wrote off $130 million for an ERP project that has never been completed.

(continued)

Table 5.3 (*cont.*)

Year	Firm	ERP Provider/ System	Problem	Impact/Result
2002 (started 1998)	PharmaCo	Oracle and Riamb Software Tech.	The company was not prepared for the implementation. Managers did not fully understand that implementing ERP involved BPR.	project ended with $850,000; after 8 months, PharmaCo restarted the ERP project and Oracle closed business partnership with Chinese service provider.
2003	British Sky Broadcasting	EDS	Project being poorly specified further down the line. BSB has alleged that EDS dishonestly exaggerated its abilities and resources when bidding for the contract.	Resulting in late delivery of the project and lost benefits that made up the £709 million.
2004	HP	mySAP ERP	Contingency planning was not addressed properly; data integration issues; demand forecasting problems.	The project eventually cost HP $160 million in order backlogs and lost revenue—more than five times the project's estimated cost.
2005 (started 2003)	Overstock	Oracle	System didn't hook up some of the accounting wiring causing billing errors.	Reduced revenues over a five-and-a-half-year period to the second quarter of 2008 by $12.9 million and a net loss of $10.3 million.
2006	Whaley Foodservice Repairs	Epicor	The ERP system was not flexible enough to make the customizations.	Epicor estimated that the implementation would cost $190,000, while the actual implementation cost ended up exceeding $1 million. The company wasn't able to use the system as expected after two years in production, requiring additional work and costs.

Year	Company	Vendor		
2007	American LaFrance	IBM Corp.	When the new system was switched on reports, it caused that production was thrown into chaos resulting in disruption to cash flow and ultimately a liquidity crisis.	ALF became unable to complete the manufacture of many pre-ordered vehicles and in effect it caused bankruptcy.
2008 (started 2005)	Waste Management	SAP AG	SAP delivered an older version than those assumed in the negotiations; the system was not adapted to company processes.	Company claimed it suffered significant damages, including more than $100 million spent on the project, as well as more than $350 million for benefits it would have gained if the software had worked as intended.
2009 (started 2007)	Shane Co. Jewelry	SAP AG	Time and cost of implementation increased from one year and $10 million to three years and $36 million; nine months of inventory issues that adversely affected sales.	Company experienced a 32% decline in sales during the holiday season which led to the brink of bankruptcy (founder borrowed money from a separate business).
2010 (started 1998)	New York's CityTime	SAIC	Trouble with understanding how complex is the project; massive corruption and waste in project management.	Originally budgeted at around US$60 million, raised to a colossal $700 million-plus USD.
2011	ParknPool	Epicor	Software couldn't process orders and doubled commission payments for sales representatives.	The company valued the cost of the failed implementation at $250,000.

(continued)

Table 5.3 *(cont.)*

Year	Firm	ERP Provider/ System	Problem	Impact/Result
2012	NCC Group	SAP	Upon going live, the new system caused immediate and significant disruption to the group. The solution significantly impaired, rather than improved, business efficiency.	Revert to an old, group-wide IT system from Sage; company had to write off £6.9 million in the final year of implementation, which includes the expected £900,000 cash cost of reverting back to the old system.
2013 (started 2009)	Bridgestone	IBM	System lost or deleted scheduled customer orders; it didn't process orders properly—duplicated them, or partially processed; for those orders that were processed, did not complete critical corresponding business application.	Bridgestone claimed more than $200 million in lost revenue and extra costs. Implementation costs: $75 million.
2014 (started 2012)	National Grid Gas Company	SAP	Inaccurate wage payments to unpaid vendor bills.	The original implementation ($400 million), along with fixing the software, brought the total cost of the system to nearly $1 billion.

Source: Authors' own elaboration based on Supply Chain Digest 2006; Chickowski, May 2009; Chickowski, April 2009; Ciecierski 2011; Duvall 2016; Kanaracus 2010, 2008; Kim 2014; Kimberling, January 2011, September 2011, 2012; Koch, June 2004; July 2004; Krigsman 2008, 2011, 2013; Lewis 2013; Nguyen 2012; Wailgum 2009; Wolfe 2008; Worthen 2002; Xuea 2005.

existing processes, or together with the implementation the processes will be evolved should be preceded by the analysis of the impact of changes on the operation. Needs should be determined as accurately as possible. It is recommended to prepare maps for the whole process, indicating the information needs of each activity and the needs for integration with other systems. Scrupulous preparation for the consultation phase will affect the accuracy of initial valuation, comparing the capabilities of different systems and making an analysis of the hardware needs. Selecting a system should also explore the possibility of its evolution, together with the company and the possibility of exchange of information in the supply chain. Modern ERP systems are modular solutions, but these are configured by size and type of companies as well as the type of the software (on-premise, Cloud ERP, SaaS). The choice of a particular solution will have a bearing not only on potential development but on the price of implementation and service. It is important, that all these elements are considered as factors in ERP system selection.

2. Select a project team and prepare a realistic implementation project.
   A well-prepared functional scope of implementation and range of changes in business processes are crucial factors for adjustments to the budget and schedule. Prepared documents should be reviewed by the project team, which includes the representatives of the vendor and delegated company members of higher and lower management directly connected with processes in which changes will occur. The work schedule should not be forcibly accelerated and subordinated to other events affecting the functioning of the company. Nor should it be artificially lengthened, either. Project implementation should take into account available resources of the company, the supplier of equipment and the provider of IT solutions, testing time (selecting the optimal testing method) and training time.

3. Skillfully manage the change.
   ERP implementation is often associated with redesigning processes (necessary or voluntary) that, together with the new system, is a major change for employees. This applies both to senior management and operational staff. Unwillingness to change and lack of commitment are often the biggest barriers to implementation. For this reason, it is so important to involve the employees and inform them about the change process before the project begins and throughout its course. Employees should be part of the changes, on one hand to report problems and suggestions of solutions at the stage of identifying needs, and on the other hand during the implementation to support the project team in agreeing to new responsibilities. Also extremely

important is organization of the testing and training processes. Training should include a discussion of changes in the process, introduction to the workplace and verification after tests.

ERP implementation usually present serious cost and organizational challenges for the company. Organizations cannot afford to fail and that is why it is so important to derive insights from the experience of previous implementations. Here. careful and thoughtful decisions are the key to success.

Conclusion

ERP systems are evolving to meet business needs. Vendors offer increasingly complex solutions that are able to support the companies from different industries and integrate all information and processes in the company area and its environment. Unfortunately, ERP systems are not always successfully implemented in many companies. Despite the existing ERP implementation methodologies, experiences of the ERP vendors, advanced facilities of the systems, a huge number of implementations failed, caused irreversible effects for enterprises. Therefore, it is very important to realize the risk, costs and changes that are connected with the implementation.

As shown in the presented case studies, the costs of implementing ERP software involving the planning, configuration, customization, testing, training and developing the infrastructure and so forth are very high. Time frames required for implementing ERP often take several years. Inappropriate process design in the implemented system and problems with system's customization causes problems with applicability of the system. The end users misunderstanding of the changes implemented with ERP is a considerable blocking factor.

This are only few facts that confirmed that decision about implementing an ERP system, preparation for the planned change and finally the implementation must be balanced, well-structured and built on the basis of a common understanding between ERP consultants (vendors) and company managers. No one plans to fail, but it is important to make sure that the operation can survive the failure of a project.

References

Abramek, Edyta Sołtysik-Piorunkiewicz, Anna, Sroka, Henryk (2014). *Kierunki badań i perspektywy rozwoju zintegrowanych systemów informatycznych zarządzania, Business Informatics 1/ 31*. Wrocław: Wydawnictwo Uniwersytetu Ekonomicznego we Wrocławiu, 114–25.

Antero, Michelle Carol (2015). *A Multi-Case Analysis of the Development of Enterprise Resource Planning Systems (ERP) Business Practices.* PhD Series 06. Copenhagen: Copenhagen Business School http://openarchive.cbs.dk/bitstream/handle/10398/9118/Michelle_Antero.pdf?sequence=1.

Burnson, Forrest (2016). What is postmodern ERP? http://www.softwareadvice.com/resources/postmodern-erp-defined/.

Chickowski, Ericka (2009). ERP hell. May 15 http://www.baselinemag.com/c/a/IT-Management/Projects-Gone-Wrong-234902/3.

——— (2009). Five ERP disasters explained. April 6 http://www.baselinemag.com/c/a/ERP/Five-ERP-Disasters-Explained-878312.

Ciecierski, Anya (2011). ERP customer sues Epicor for project inflated to $1 million. September 26 http://www.erpsoftwareblog.com/2011/09/erp-customer-sues-epicor-for-project-inflated-to-1-million/.

Columbus, Louis (2014). Gartner's ERP market share update shows the future of Cloud ERP is now. May 12 http://www.forbes.com/sites/louiscolumbus/2014/05/12/gartners-erp-market-share-update-shows-the-future-of-cloud-erp-is-now/#7c8a91e474a1

Computer Profile (2015). The ERP solution from SAP is used most by Dutch companies. March http://www.computerprofile.com/analytics-papers/the-erp-solution-from-sap-is-used-most-by-dutch-companies/

Duvall, M. (n.d.) ERP errors lead Overstock.com to restate earnings. http://www.ciozone.com/index.php/Tools/ERP-Errors-Lead-Overstock.com-To-Restate-Earnings.html.

Focus Research ERP Group (2009). ERP Systems market primer. May http://www.alticoadvisors.com/Portals/0/ERP-Market-Primer-28may09.pdf.

Ghosh, Rittik (2012). "A comprehensive study on ERP failures stressing on reluctance to change as a cause of failure." *Journal of Marketing and Management*, 3(1): 123–34.

IT Polska News (2014). Raport ERP, June 23 http://www.itpolska-news.pl/raport-wszystko-o-erp/.

Jacobs, F. Robert and Weston Jr., F. C. (2007). Enterprise resource planning (ERP): A brief history. *Journal of Operations Management* 25: 357–63.

Kalaimani, Jayaraman. (2016). *SAP Project Management Pitfalls.* New York: Apress.

Kanaracus, Chris (2008). Waste Management sues SAP over ERP implementation. March 27 http://www.computerworld.com/article/2536212/enterprise-applications/waste-management-sues-sap-over-erp-implementation.html.

——— . (2010). Biggest ERP failures of 2010. December 28 http://www.infoworld.com/article/2624762/erp/biggest-erp-failures-of-2010.html.

Kim, Eugene (2014). A troubled project to replace Oracle with SAP software could cost a New York gas utility nearly $1 billion. October 6 http://www.businessinsider.com/national-grid-sap-1-billion-upgrade-cost-2014-10?IR=T.

Kimberling, Eric (2011). ERP failures and lawsuits: It's not just for the Tier I ERP vendors. January 12 http://panorama-consulting.com/erp-failures-and-lawsuits-its-not-just-for-the-tier-i-erp-vendors/.

——— . What was the cause of the recent Epicor ERP implementation failure and lawsuit? September 19 http://panorama-consulting.com/what-was-the-cause-of-the-recent-epicor-erp-implementation-failure-and-lawsuit/.

——— . (2012). Lessons from New York City: The risks and benefits of hiring outside ERP consultants. April 18 http://panorama-consulting.com/lessons-from-new-york-city-the-risks-and-benefits-of-hiring-outside-erp-consultants/.

Koch, Christopher (2004). Nike rebounds: How (and why) Nike recovered from its supply chain disaster. June 15 http://www.cio.com/article/2439601/supply-chain-management/nike-rebounds--how--and-why--nike-recovered-from-its-supply-chain-disaster.html.

————. (2004). SCM and ERP software implementation at Nike: From failure to success. July 25 http://www.icmrindia.org/casestudies/catalogue/Operations/SCM%20and%20ERP%20Software%20Implementation%20at%20Nike-From%20Failure%20to%20Success.htm.

Krigsman, Michael (2008). Customer blames bankruptcy on IBM IT failure. June 16 http://www.ciozone.com/index.php/Tools/ERP-Errors-Lead-Overstock.com-To-Restate-Earnings.html.

————. (2011). ERP train wrecks, failures, and lawsuits. January 19 http://www.zdnet.com/article/erp-train-wrecks-failures-and-lawsuits/.

————. (2013). PR finger pointing: IBM and Bridgestone wrangle over failed ERP. November 29 http://www.zdnet.com/article/pr-finger-pointing-ibm-and-bridgestone-wrangle-over-failed-erp/.

Krupa, Marian (2016). Metodyka wdrożenia zintegrowanego oprogramowania biznesowego w teorii i w praktyce zarządzania polskich przedsiębiorstw. June, downloadable http://slideplayer.pl/slide/428662/.

Lewis, Abbie (2013). The top three ERP implementation disasters. November 27 http://www.sharedserviceslink.com/blog/the-top-three-truly-shocking-erp-implementation-disasters.

Lutovac, Miroslav (2012). "The successful methodology for enterprise resource planning (ERP) implementation," *Journal of Modern Accounting and Auditing* 8(12): 1838–47.

Møller, Charles (2016). ERP II: Next-generation extended enterprise resource planning. June, downloadable http://pure.au.dk/portal/files/32334597/0003167.pdf.

Nguyen, Anh (2012). NCC Group reverts to Sage following failed SAP implementation. June 1 http://www.computerworlduk.com/news/it-management/ncc-group-reverts-sage-following-failed-sap-implementation-3361471/.

Panorama Consulting Solutions, 2012 ERP Report, 2012, 1–22.

————., 2013 ERP Report, 2013, 2–21.

————., 2014 ERP Report, 2014, 1–18.

————., 2015 ERP Report, 2015, 1–17.

————., 2016 Report on ERP Systems and Enterprise Software, 2016, 2–30.

Patil, Nileema B., Samel, Madhuri, Tilak, Priya and Boban, Dolly (2015). "Evolution of modern enterprise resource planning (ERP) systems on technological background." *International Journal of Science and Research (IJSR)*, 4(1): 1255–57.

SAP (2016): ASAP 8 methodology for implementation. June, https://support.sap.com/support-programs-services/methodologies/implement-sap/asap-implementation.html.

Salimi, Farshad (2005). *ERP Implementation Methodologies: Differences in ERP Implementation between Manufacturing and Services*. Rotterdam: The Printer BV.

SupplyChainDigest (2006). The 11 greatest supply chain disasters, 1–12. http://www.scdigest.com/assets/reps/SCDigest_Top-11-SupplyChainDisasters.pdf.

Wailgum, Thomas (2009). Ten famous ERP disasters, dustups and disappointments. March 24 http://www.cio.com/article/2429865/enterprise-resource-planning/10-famous-erp-disasters--dustups-and-disappointments.html.

Wolfe, Kenneth L. (2008). ERP implementation failure at Hershey Foods Corporation, ICAFI Center for Management Research (ICMR), 2–12, http://www.academia.edu/4630187/ERP_Implementation_Failure_Hershey_Foods_Corporation.

Wood, Bill (2010). ERP vs. ERP II vs. ERP III Future Enterprise Applications. May 31 http://www.r3now.com/erp-vs-erp-ii-vs-erp-iii-future-enterprise-applications/.

Worthen, Ben (2002). Nestlé's Enterprise Resource Planning (ERP) odyssey. May 15 http://www.cio.com/article/2440821/enterprise-resource-planning/nestl--s-enterprise-resource-planning--erp--odyssey.html.

Xue, Yajiong, Liangb, Huigang, Boultonc, William R., Snyderc, Charles A. (2005). ERP implementation failures in China: Case studies with implications for ERP vendors. *International Journal of Production Economics* 97, 279–95.

Lightning Source UK Ltd.
Milton Keynes UK
UKHW01n0942310518
323505UK00009B/314/P